PIETA OF THE APOCALYPSE

Essential End Time Prayers and Promises

Mother and Refuge

Mother and Refuge of the End TImes Books

ISBN: 9798816841375

Cover design by: Ron Ray
Printed in the United States of America

The contents of this book are a combination of prayers from the public domain and content used with the permission of the following:
The Marian Fathers of the Immaculate Conception of the BVM, Stockbridge, MA USA
The Association of the Precious Blood of Jesus (PreciousBloodInternational.com)
Blue Army Press (bluearmy.com)
After the Warning website (AfterTheWarning.com)
The Flame of Love website (flameoflove.us)

CONTENTS

PREFACE

Dear Readers of "Pieta of the Apocalypse",

This PRAYER BOOK is so rich in content! It contains all the important devotions of the Catholic Church given by Jesus and Our Blessed Mother through saints and mystics.
I BLESS THIS BOOKLET AND RECOMMEND IT TO EVERYBODY.

GOD BLESS YOU ALL.

Rev. Fr. Francis M. Kumi (OSB)

Note to the Reader: The author of this book claims no authority to judge the final veracity of any particular apparition or locution and leaves final judgement to the authority of the Church.

INTRODUCTION

Dear readers, we thank you for your love and support of the 'Mother and Refuge of the End Times' ministry. This prayer book has been inspired by the prophetic messages that have been posted on our YouTube channel.

We are well aware of the lateness of the hour, and we would like to equip you for this time of pain and tribulation with this little book of treasures from heaven.

The prayers in this book have been given to catholic end time seers and mystics over the last century or more. Our Lord Jesus and His Blessed Mother Mary have warned us of the apocalyptic times that we are now facing. They have also blessed us with an abundance of grace filled devotions to assist us through this valley of tears.

Therefore, all the prayers in this book have been directly given to us by heaven for our help and assistance in these end times.

We pray that this prayerbook may be with its faithful owner throughout these difficult times and be a tool to aide the reader in lifting his or her soul up to heaven. It is thus, a prayer book for the refuges of the Great Tribulation.

We ask the Lord that this book of end time prayers be for you a means of reaching the spiritual refuge of the Immaculate Heart of Mary and Sacred Heart of Jesus.

ABOUT THE TITLE *"THE PIETA OF THE APOCALYPSE"*

As we behold the Body of Our Lord Jesus in the arms of His loving Mother in the Pieta, today, we also reflect upon the lifeless Body of Christ, the Church, in the arms of Our Blessed Mother Mary. Our Lady holds the Church close to Her Immaculate Heart as it journeys through its own 'Way of the Cross'. In the arms of Our Lady, we too hold firm hope that the Church, the Mystical Body of Christ, will soon experience its rebirth and resurrection like its Master. As the Church experiences its painful and sorrowful Calvary, we who stand close to Our Blessed Mother, are eagerly awaiting a promised Era of Peace. We also await the triumph of the Eucharistic Jesus in a united and renewed Church that imitates the Lord in all things. Thus, the 'Pieta of the Apocalypse' is a fitting depiction for this book.

CHAPTER 1 – FATIMA & THE FLAME OF LOVE OF THE IMMACULATE HEART OF MARY - SEER ELIZABETH KINDELMANN

T
he Flame of Love of the Immaculate Heart of Mary is intrinsically connected to Our Lady of Fatima and the call for devotion to the Immaculate Heart above all through the recitation of the Holy Rosary and the practice of the first five Saturdays devotion. Our Lady said, *"I promise to assist at the moment of death, with all the graces necessary for salvation, those who on the first Saturday of five consecutive months, shall confess, receive Holy Communion, recite five decades of the*

Rosary, and keep me company for fifteen minutes while meditating on the fifteen mysteries of the Rosary with the intention of making reparation to me."

Requirements of the Five First Saturday Reparation

Every catholic could fulfill this request by going an hour early to the Saturday vigil mass, saying **The Holy Rosary**, going to confession (almost always available before the vigil mass), meditating for fifteen minutes on the mysteries of the Rosary, receiving Holy Communion, and fulfilling these four conditions in reparation for the offenses committed against the Immaculate Heart.

How to Pray The Holy Rosary

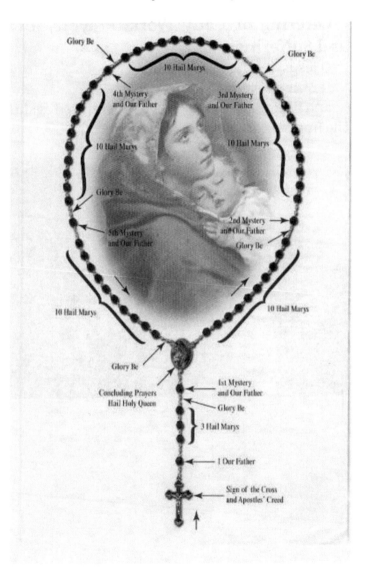

Glory Be

Glory Be

10 Hail Marys

4th Mystery and Our Father

3rd Mystery and Our Father

10 Hail Marys

10 Hail Marys

Glory Be

2nd Mystery and Our Father

5th Mystery and Our Father

Glory Be

10 Hail Marys

10 Hail Marys

Glory Be

1st Mystery and Our Father

Concluding Prayers Hail Holy Queen

Glory Be

3 Hail Marys

1 Our Father

Sign of the Cross and Apostles' Creed

Fatima Prayers

Offering of Daily Work, Prayers, Joys, and Sufferings

O Jesus, it is for love of Thee,
for the conversion of sinners,
and in reparation for the sins committed against the Immaculate Heart of Mary.

Pardon Prayer

My God, I believe, I adore,
I trust and I love You!
And I beg pardon for all those who do not believe,
who do not adore, who do not trust and who do
not love You.

*Delivered by the Angel of Peace during the first apparition of the angel to the three shepherd children of Fatima in the spring of 1916.

Angel's Prayer

O Most Holy Trinity, Father, Son and Holy Spirit, I adore Thee profoundly. I offer Thee the most precious Body, Blood, Soul and Divinity of Jesus Christ present in all the tabernacles of the world, in reparation for the outrages, sacrileges and indifferences by which He Himself is offended. And by the infinite merits of His Most Sacred Heart and the Immaculate Heart of Mary, I beg of Thee the conversion of poor sinners.

*Delivered by the Angel of Peace during the third apparition of the Angel in October 1916. The Angel appeared to the three shepherd children holding a chalice in his hands, with a Host above it from which drops of Blood were falling into the chalice.

Decade Prayer

O My Jesus, forgive us our sins, save us from the fires of hell. Lead all souls to Heaven, especially those most in need of Thy mercy. Amen.

*Delivered by Our Lady during the Third Apparition of Our Lady of Fatima to the three shepherd children on July 13, 1917. Traditionally prayed after the 'Glory Be' for each decade of the Rosary.

Prayer Before The Rosary

Queen of the Holy Rosary, you have deigned to come to Fatima to reveal to the three shepherd children the treasures of grace hidden in the Rosary. Inspire my heart with a sincere love of this devotion, in order that by meditating on the Mysteries of our Redemption, which are recalled in it, I may be enriched with its fruits and obtain peace for the world, the conversion of sinners and of Russia, and the favor which I ask of you in this Rosary. (Here mention your request.) I ask it for the greater glory of God, for your own honor, and for the good of souls, especially for my own. Amen.

Vision of Sister Lucia, Seer of Fatima, in 1926

Words of Sister Lucia: Suddenly the whole chapel was illumined by supernatural light, and above the alter appeared a cross of light, reaching to the ceiling. In a brighter light at the upper part of the cross, could be seen the face of a Man and His body as far as the waist; upon His breast was a dove of light; nailed to the cross was the body of another Man. A little below the waist, I could see a chalice and a large Host suspended in the air, on to which drops of Blood were falling from the face of Jesus Crucified and from the wound in His side. These drops ran down on to the Host and fell into the chalice.

Beneath the right arm of the cross was Our Lady and in Her hand was Her Immaculate Heart. (It was Our Lady of Fatima, with Her Immaculate Heart in Her left hand, without sword or roses, but with a crown of thorns and flames). Under the left arm of the cross, large letters, as if of crystal clear water which ran down upon the altar, formed these words: "**Grace and Mercy**".

Promises of the Flame of Love of the Immaculate Heart of Mary

Elizabeth Kindelmann wrote: "I am going to record what the Blessed Virgin told me in [October of] this year, 1962. I kept it inside for a long time without daring to write it down. It is a petition of the Blessed Virgin: 'When you say the prayer that honors me, the Hail Mary, include this petition in the following manner:

Hail Mary, full of grace ... pray for us sinners, spread the effect of grace of thy Flame of Love over all of humanity, now and at the hour of our death. Amen.'"

The bishop asked Elizabeth: "Why should the very old Hail Mary be recited differently?" "On February 2, 1982, Our Lord explained, 'Because of the Holy Virgin's efficacious pleas, the Most Blessed Trinity granted the outpouring of the Flame of Love. For her sake, you must place this prayer in the Hail Mary so that, by its effect, humanity is converted.' Our Lady also said, 'I want to awaken humanity by this petition. This is not a new formula but a constant supplication. If at any moment, someone prays three Hail Mary's in my honor, while referring to the Flame of Love, they will free a soul from purgatory. During November, one Hail Mary will free ten souls.'"

"On August 31, 1963, ... as I interceded for the souls in purgatory, Our Lady spoke; 'I value your longing for the souls in purgatory. Until now, you had to say 3 Hail Marys. In the future, three Hail Marys will free ten souls from that place of suffering." (Source: https://flameoflove.us/)

(Elizabeth Kindelmann and the Shroud
Image of the Holy Face)

The Unity Prayer

Jesus said: "I made this prayer completely My own ... This prayer is an instrument in your hands. By collaborating with Me, Satan will be blinded by it; and because of his blindness, souls will not be led into sin.

May our feet journey together.

May our hands gather in unity.

May our hearts beat in unison.

May our souls be in harmony.

May our thoughts be as one.

May our ears listen to the silence together.

May our glances profoundly penetrate each other.

May our lips pray together to gain mercy from the Eternal Father."

On August 1, 1962, three months after Our Lord introduced the Unity Prayer, Our Lady said to Elizabeth: "Now, Satan has been blinded for some hours and has ceased dominating souls. Lust is the sin making so many victims. Because Satan is now powerless and blind, the evil spirits are set and inert, as if they have fallen into lethargy. They do not understand what is happening. Satan has stopped giving them orders. Consequently, souls are freed from the domination of the evil one and are making sound resolutions. Once those millions of souls emerge from this event, they will be much stronger in their resolve to stay firm."

CHAPTER 2 – THE DIVINE MERCY & SAINT FAUSTINA

The Promises of Divine Mercy

The Divine Mercy Chaplet was presented to St. Faustina in 1935 during a private revelation. Jesus asks that we meditate upon His Passion at three o'clock. The Divine Mercy Chaplet is an especially powerful way to do so.

Here Are14 Promises Jesus Made To Those Who Pray The Divine Mercy Chaplet:

1) "I promise that the soul that will venerate this image (of Divine Mercy) will not perish. I also promise victory over (its) enemies already here on earth, especially at the hour of death. I Myself will defend it as My own glory."
(*Diary of St. Faustina,* 48)

2) "The two rays denote Blood and Water... These two rays issued from the very depths of My tender mercy when My agonized Heart was opened by a lance on the Cross. These rays shield souls from the wrath of My Father...I desire that the first Sunday after Easter be the Feast of Mercy...whoever approaches the Fount of Life on this day will be granted complete remission of sins and punishment. Mankind will not have peace until it turns with trust to My mercy."
(*Diary of St. Faustina,* 299-300)

3) "I desire that the Feast of Mercy...be solemnly celebrated on the first Sunday after Easter...The soul that will go to Confession and receive Holy Communion (in a state of grace on this day) shall obtain complete forgiveness of sins and punishment."

(Diary of St. Faustina, 699)

4) **"Whoever will recite it will receive great mercy at the hour of death."**
(Diary of St. Faustina, 687)

5) **"Priests will recommend it to sinners as their last hope of salvation. Even if there were a sinner most hardened, if he were to recite this chaplet only once, he would receive grace from My infinite mercy...I desire to grant unimaginable graces to those souls who trust in My mercy."**
(Diary of St. Faustina, 687)

6) **"The souls that say this chaplet will be embraced by My mercy during their lifetime and especially at the hour of their death."**
(Diary of St. Faustina, 754)

7) **"Souls who spread the honor of My mercy...at the hour of death I will not be a Judge for them, but the Merciful Savior."**
(Diary of St. Faustina, 1075)

8) **"The prayer most pleasing to Me is prayer for the conversion for sinners. Know, my daughter, that this prayer is always heard and answered."**
(Diary of St. Faustina, 1397)

9) **"My mercy is greater than your sins and those of the entire world."** *(Diary of St. Faustina,*

1485)

10) "**To priests who proclaim and extol My mercy, I will give wondrous power; I will anoint their words and touch the hearts of those to whom they will speak.**"
(*Diary of St. Faustina,* 1521)

11) "**Through this chaplet you will obtain everything, if what you ask for is compatible with My will.**"
(*Diary of St. Faustina,* 1731)

12) "**When hardened sinners say it, I will fill their souls with peace, and the hour of their death will be a happy one.**"
(*Diary of St. Faustina,* 1541)

13) "**When they say this chaplet in the presence of the dying, I will stand between My Father and the dying person, not as a just Judge but as a merciful Savior.**"
(*Diary of St. Faustina,* 1541)

14) "**At three o'clock, implore My mercy, especially for sinners; and, if only for a brief moment, immerse yourself in My Passion, particularly in My abandonment at the moment of agony...I will refuse nothing to the soul that makes a request of Me in virtue of My Passion.**"
(*Diary of St. Faustina,* 1320)
(Source: https://fathersofmercy.com)

The Divine Mercy Chaplet

1) Opening

Sign of the Cross

In the name of the Father, and of the Son, and of the Holy Spirit. Amen.

First opening prayer (optional)

You expired, Jesus, but the source of life gushed forth for souls, and the ocean of mercy opened up for the whole world. O Fount of Life, unfathomable Divine Mercy, envelop the whole world and empty Yourself out upon us.

Second opening prayer (optional) (x3)

O Blood and Water, which gushed forth from the Heart of Jesus as a fountain of Mercy for us, I trust in You.

Our Father

Our Father, who art in heaven, hallowed by thy name. Thy kingdom come, thy will be done,
On earth as it is in heaven.
Give us this day our daily bread,
And forgive us our trespasses as we forgive those who trespass against us.
And lead us not into temptation,
But deliver us from evil. Amen.

Hail Mary

Hail, Mary, full of grace, the Lord is with thee.
Blessed art thou among women,
And blessed is the fruit of thy womb Jesus.
Holy Mary, mother of God, pray for us sinners,
Now and at the hour of our death. Amen.

Apostles' Creed

I believe in God,
the Father almighty,
Creator of heaven and earth,
and in Jesus Christ, his only Son, our Lord,
who was conceived by the Holy Spirit,
born of the Virgin Mary,
suffered under Pontius Pilate,
was crucified, died and was buried;
he descended into hell;
on the third day he rose again from the dead;
he ascended into heaven,
and is seated at the right hand of God the Father
almighty;
from there he will come to judge the living and the
dead.
I believe in the Holy Spirit,
the holy catholic Church,
the communion of saints,
the forgiveness of sins,
the resurrection of the body,

and life everlasting. Amen.

2) Decades (x5)

Eternal Father

Eternal Father, I offer you the body and blood, soul and divinity of your dearly beloved Son, Our Lord, Jesus Christ, in atonement for our sins and those of the whole world.

For the sake of His sorrowful passion (x10)

For the sake of His sorrowful passion, have mercy on us and on the whole world.

3) Closing

Holy God (x3)

Holy God, Holy Mighty One, Holy Immortal One, have mercy on us and on the whole world.

Closing Prayer (Optional)

Eternal God, in whom mercy is endless and the treasury of compassion inexhaustible, look kindly upon us and increase Your mercy in us, that in difficult moments we might not despair nor become despondent, but with great confidence submit ourselves to Your holy will which is Love and Mercy itself.

Sign of the Cross

In the name of the Father, and of the Son, and of the Holy Spirit. Amen.

4) Litany of Divine Mercy

Divine Mercy, gushing forth from the bosom of the Father, **I trust in You.**

Divine Mercy, greatest attribute of GOD, **I trust in You.**

Divine Mercy, incomprehensible mystery, **I trust in You.**

Divine Mercy, fountain gushing forth from the mystery of the Most Blessed Trinity, **I trust in You.**

Divine Mercy, unfathomed by any intellect, human or angelic, **I trust in You.**

Divine Mercy, from which wells forth all life and happiness, **I trust in You.**

Divine Mercy, better than the heavens, **I trust in You.**

Divine Mercy, source of miracles and wonders, **I**

trust in You.

Divine Mercy, encompassing the whole universe, **I trust in You.**

Divine Mercy, descending to earth in the Person of the Incarnate Word, **I trust in You.**

Divine Mercy, which flowed out from the open wound of the Heart of JESUS, **I trust in You.**

Divine Mercy, enclosed in the Heart of JESUS for us, and especially for sinners, **I trust in You**.

Divine Mercy, unfathomed in the institution of the Sacred Host, **I trust in You.**

Divine Mercy, in the founding of Holy Church, **I trust in You.**

Divine Mercy, in the Sacrament of Holy Baptism, **I trust in You.**

Divine Mercy, in our justification through JESUS CHRIST, **I trust in You.**

Divine Mercy, accompanying us through our whole life, **I trust in You**.

Divine Mercy, embracing us especially at the hour of death, **I trust in You.**

Divine Mercy, endowing us with immortal life, **I trust in You.**

Divine Mercy, accompanying us every moment of our life, **I trust in You.**

Divine Mercy, shielding us from the fire of hell, **I trust in You.**

Divine Mercy, in the conversion of hardened sinners, **I trust in You.**

Divine Mercy, astonishment for Angels,

incomprehensible to Saints, **I trust in You.**

Divine Mercy, unfathomed in all the mysteries of GOD, **I trust in You.**

Divine Mercy, lifting us out of every misery, **I trust in You.**

Divine Mercy, source of our happiness and joy, **I trust in You.**

Divine Mercy, in calling us forth from nothingness to existence, **I trust in You.**

Divine Mercy, embracing all the works of His hands, **I trust in You.**

Divine Mercy, crown of all of God's handiwork, **I trust in You.**

Divine Mercy, in which we are all immersed, **I trust in You.**

Divine Mercy, sweet relief for anguished hearts, **I trust in You.**

Divine Mercy, only hope of despairing souls, **I trust in You.**

Divine Mercy, repose of hearts, peace amidst fear, **I trust in You.**

Divine Mercy, delight and ecstasy of holy souls, **I trust in You.**

Divine Mercy, inspiring hope against all hope, **I trust in You.**

Eternal GOD, in whom mercy is endless and the treasury of compassion inexhaustible, look kindly upon us and increase Your mercy in us, that in difficult moments we might not despair nor become despondent, but with great confidence submit ourselves to Your holy will, which is Love and Mercy itself. Amen.

(St Faustina Recieves the Gift of Divine Mercy)

CHAPTER 3 – THE
CHAPLET OF PROVISION
& SEER ENOCH OF
COLOMBIA

The Promise: Pray the Rosary of Provision for Times of Scarcity and Famine!

On April the 5th, 2020 Jesus revealed to Seer Enoch of Colombia the following:

"My Peace and the Joy of my Holy Spirit, be with you all.

My Beloveds, I am your Jesus of Mercy who today communicates with you, through this, my little Prophet. Don't be afraid, my People. I will not forsake you, remember that I am with you until the end of time; follow my instructions and put them into practice; and I assure you that nothing, no one, no viruses, no plagues, no catastrophes, no famine, or any other calamity will be able to touch you.

Pray with faith, my Rosary of Mercy (Chaplet of Divine Mercy), ask for my protection and fear not; my Rays of Mercy will protect you and keep you from all evil and danger. I ask you: why are you afraid, if I am with you? Where is your faith and trust in Me? If you were men of faith, you would feel no fear, and nothing, no one, could steal your Peace. Look, you are so fragile, like little children, to the slightest misfortune, you tremble with fear; and there, yes, you cry to heaven and remember Me.

I want, my little ones, that you strengthen yourselves in the faith, so that you may endure tomorrow the great trials that will come to you.

29

Fear not, if you put your faith and your trust in Me, I will be your strength that will help you overcome the trials. Prayer, fasting, and penance will strengthen you; read also my Holy Word, which is the Sword of the Spirit, so that you may confront the attacks of the evil one. The Spiritual Armor, you must wear, before entering every combat; prayer, fasting and penance, together with the prayer of my Mother's Holy Rosary and the prayer of my Rosary of Mercy, should never be lacking.

My beloved People, My Rosary of Mercy, next to the Rosary of Provision, will be of great help to you for the times of scarcity and famine that are approaching. Pray them with faith, and ask for my provision and heaven, will bring you the everyday Manna.

Again, I tell you, fear not. I am your Refuge, Sustenance, Protection, and above all, I am your God. Come to me, all you who labor and are burdened, and I will give you rest. (Matthew 11:28)

The Prayer of the Chaplet of Provision

Opening Prayers
(For times of scarcity and famine)

"O infinite Mercy of God, which you provide to men of good will, to those in need, to widows and orphans, covering their material and spiritual needs; Open the pantries of heaven and in the Name of the Father, (blessing) in the Name of the Son, (blessing) and in the name of the Holy Spirit, (blessing) send me the provision I need to accomplish my needs of this day (make request).

Followed by one Creed and one Our Father."

On the big beads say: *I can have grace and mercy even in times of need. (Hebrews 4, 16)*

On the small beads say: *In the name of God One and Triune, Divine Mercy, provide for me. (**10 times**)*

At the end of each decade, pray: 1 Our Father and you start as in the beginning for the 5 decades of the rosary beads.

I can have grace and mercy... and so on until the end of the five decades.

At the end of the rosary, five decades, pray:

PSALM 136

Psalm 136: GOD'S WORK IN CREATION AND IN HISTORY

[1] O give thanks to the Lord, for he is good,
for his steadfast love endures forever.
[2] O give thanks to the God of gods,
for his steadfast love endures forever.
[3] O give thanks to the Lord of lords,
for his steadfast love endures forever;
[4] who alone does great wonders,
for his steadfast love endures forever;
[5] who by understanding made the heavens,
for his steadfast love endures forever;
[6] who spread out the earth on the waters,
for his steadfast love endures forever;
[7] who made the great lights,
for his steadfast love endures forever;
[8] the sun to rule over the day,
for his steadfast love endures forever;
[9] the moon and stars to rule over the night,
for his steadfast love endures forever;
[10] who struck Egypt through their firstborn,
for his steadfast love endures forever;
[11] and brought Israel out from among them,
for his steadfast love endures forever;
[12] with a strong hand and an outstretched arm,
for his steadfast love endures forever;
[13] who divided the Red Sea in two,
for his steadfast love endures forever;

[14] and made Israel pass through the midst of it,
　　for his steadfast love endures forever;
[15] but overthrew Pharaoh and his army in the Red Sea,
　　for his steadfast love endures forever;
[16] who led his people through the wilderness,
　　for his steadfast love endures forever;
[17] who struck down great kings,
　　for his steadfast love endures forever;
[18] and killed famous kings,
　　for his steadfast love endures forever;
[19] Sihon, king of the Amorites,
　　for his steadfast love endures forever;
[20] and Og, king of Bashan,
　　for his steadfast love endures forever;
[21] and gave their land as a heritage,
　　for his steadfast love endures forever;
[22] a heritage to his servant Israel,
　　for his steadfast love endures forever.
　[23] It is he who remembered us in our low estate,
　　for his steadfast love endures forever;
[24] and rescued us from our foes,
　　for his steadfast love endures forever;
[25] who gives food to all flesh,
　　for his steadfast love endures forever.
　[26] O give thanks to the God of heaven,
　　for his steadfast love endures forever.

C. SMALL BEADS:
In the name of
God, one and
Triune!

ROSARY
OF
PROVIDENCE

B. BIG BEADS:
I can have
grace and
mercy...

A. Opening
1. Infinite
Jesus
2. Creed
3. Our
Father

D. END PRAYER:
Psalm 136

CHAPTER 4 – THE SEVEN SORROW OF THE BLESSED VIRGIN MARY AND THE APPARITIONS OF KIBEHO, RWANDA

The Rosary of the Seven Sorrows dates back to the fourteenth century. Mary, Our Lady of Sorrows, appeared to St. Bridget of Sweden and revealed this Rosary devotion to Her. During the Marian apparitions in Kibeho, Rwanda, in the 1980s. Our Lady assigned Marie-Claire Mukangango a mission to reintroduce this special Rosary to the world. Marie-Claire was killed in the genocide of over a million people in Rwanda.

Our Lady of Kibeho said:

"There isn't much time left for preparing for the Last Judgment. We must change our lives, renounce sin. Pray and prepare for our death and for the end of the world. We must prepare while there is still time. Those who do well will go to Heaven. If they do evil, they will condemn themselves with no hope of appeal. Do not lose time in doing good and praying. There is not much time and Jesus will come."

She (The Holy Virgin) promised that when prayed with an open and repentant heart, the rosary would win us the Lord's forgiveness for our sins and free our souls from guilt and remorse. She also promised special gifts. The rosary would develop within us a deep understanding of why we sin, and that knowledge would give us the wisdom and strength to change internal flaws, weaknesses of character, or personality faults causing unhappiness and keeping us from enjoying the joyous life God intended for us...

THE ROSARY OF THE SEVEN SORROWS OF MARY BY OUR LADY OF KIBEHO

Sign of the Cross: *In the name of The Father, and The Son, and The Holy Spirit. Amen.*

Introductory Prayer: *My God, I offer You this Rosary for Your glory, so I can honor your Holy Mother, the Blessed Virgin, so I can share and meditate upon her suffering. I humbly beg you to give me true repentance for all my sins. Give me wisdom and humility, so that I may receive all the indulgences contained in this prayer.*

Act of Contrition: *O my God, I am heartily sorry for having offended You, and I detest all my sins because I dread the loss of Heaven and the pains of hell; but most of all because they offend You, my God, You Who are all good and deserving of all my love. I firmly resolve, with the help of Your grace, to confess my sins, to do penance, and to amend my life. Amen.* **(Pray 3 Hail Mary's)**

Most Merciful Mother, remind us always about the Sorrows of your Son, Jesus.

Seven swords pierce the Immaculate Heart of Mary

1) THE FIRST SWORD OF SORROW: THE PROPHECY OF SIMEON (LUKE 2:22-35)

"Now Your servant may depart this life in peace, my Lord," he said... Simeon blessed them and said to Mary his mother, "Behold, this Child is set for the fall and rising of many in Israel, and for a sign that is spoken against (and a sword will pierce through your own soul also), that thoughts out of many hearts may be revealed."

The Blessed Virgin knew that she had given birth to the Savior of humankind, so she immediately understood and accepted Simeon's prophecy. Although her Heart was deeply touched by this favor of bearing the Baby Jesus, her Heart remained heavy and troubled, for she knew what had been written about the ordeals and subsequent death of the Savior. Whenever she saw her Son, she was constantly reminded of the suffering He would be subject to, and His suffering became her own.

38

Prayer: *Beloved Mother Mary, whose Heart suffered beyond bearing because of us, teach us to suffer with you and with love, and to accept all the suffering God deems it necessary to send our way. Let us suffer, and may our suffering be known to God only, like yours and that of Jesus. Do not let us show our suffering to the world, so it will matter more and be used to atone for the sins of the world. You, Mother, who suffered with the Savior of the world, we offer you our suffering, and the suffering of the world, because we are your children. Join those sorrows to your own and to those of the Lord Jesus Christ, then offer them to God the Father. You are a Mother greater than all.* **(Pray 1 Our Father and 7 Hail Mary's)**

Most Merciful Mother, remind us always about the Sorrows of your Son, Jesus.

2. THE SECOND SWORD OF SORROW: THE FLIGHT INTO EGYPT (MATTHEW 2:13-15)

Mary's Heart broke and her mind was greatly troubled when Joseph revealed to her the words of the angel: they were to wake up quickly and flee to Egypt because Herod wanted to kill Jesus. The Blessed Virgin hardly had time to decide what to take or leave behind; she took her Child and left everything else, rushing outside before Joseph so that they could hurry as God wished. Then she said, "Even though God has power over everything, He wants us to flee with Jesus, His Son. God will show us the way, and we shall arrive without being caught by the enemy."

Because the Blessed Virgin was the Mother of Jesus, she loved Him more than anyone else. Her heart was deeply troubled at the sight of her Infant Son's discomfort, and she suffered greatly because He was cold and shivering. While she and her husband were tired, sleepy, and hungry during this long travel, Mary's only thought was about the safety and comfort of her Child. She feared coming face to face with the soldiers who had been ordered to kill Jesus because she was aware that the enemy was still in Bethlehem. Her heart remained constantly anguished during this flight. She also knew that where they were going, there would be no friendly faces to greet them.

Prayer: *Beloved Mother, who has suffered so much, give to us your courageous heart. Please pray for us to have strength so that we can be brave like you and accept with love the suffering God sends our way. Help us to also accept all the suffering we inflict upon* *ourselves and the suffering inflicted upon us by others. Heavenly Mother, you, in union with Jesus, purify our suffering so that we may give glory to God and save our souls.* **(Pray 1 Our Father and 7 Hail Mary's)**

Most Merciful Mother, remind us always about the Sorrows of your Son, Jesus.

3. THE THIRD SWORD OF SORROW: THE LOSS OF JESUS IN THE TEMPLE (LUKE 2:41-52)

Jesus was the only begotten Son of God, but He was also Mary's child. The Blessed Virgin loved Jesus more than herself because He was her God. Compared to other children, He was most unique because He was already living as God. When Mary lost Jesus on their way back from Jerusalem, the world became so big and lonely that she believed she couldn't go on living without Him, so great was her Sorrow. (She felt the same pain her Son felt when He was later abandoned by His apostles during the Passion.)

As the Holy Mother looked anxiously for her beloved Boy, deep pain welled in her heart. She blamed herself, asking why she didn't take greater care of Him. But it was not her fault; Jesus no longer needed her protection as before. What really hurt Mary was that her son had decided to stay behind without her consent. Jesus had pleased her in everything so far: He never annoyed her in any way, nor would He ever displease His parents. She knew that He always did what was necessary, however, so she never suspected Him of being disobedient.

Prayer: *Beloved Mother, teach us to accept all our sufferings because of our sins and to atone for the sins of the whole world.* **(Pray 1 Our Father and 7 Hail Mary's)**

Most Merciful Mother, remind us always about the Sorrows of your Son, Jesus.

4. THE FOURTH SWORD OF SORROW: MARY MEETS JESUS ON THE WAY TO CALVARY (LUKE 23:27-31)

Mary witnessed Jesus carrying the heavy cross alone—the cross on which He was to be crucified. This didn't surprise the Blessed Virgin because she already knew about the approaching death of Our Lord. Noting how her son was already weakened by the numerous hard blows given by the soldiers' clubs, she was filled with anguish at His pain. The soldiers kept hurrying and pushing Him, though He had no strength left. He fell, exhausted, unable to raise Himself. At that moment, Mary's eyes, so full of tender love and compassion, met her Son's eyes, which were pained and covered in blood. Their hearts seemed to be sharing the load; every pain He felt, she felt as well. They knew that nothing could be done except to believe and trust in God and dedicate their suffering to Him. All they could do was put everything in God's hands.

Prayer: *Beloved Mother, so stricken with grief, help us to bear our own suffering with courage and love so that we may relieve your Sorrowful Heart and that of Jesus. In doing so, may we give glory to God Who gave you and Jesus to humanity. As you suffered, teach us* *to suffer silently and patiently. Grant unto us the grace of loving God in everything. O Mother of Sorrows, most afflicted of all mothers, have mercy on the sinners of the whole world.*

(Pray 1 Our Father and 7 Hail Mary's)

Most Merciful Mother, remind us always about the Sorrows of your Son, Jesus.

5. THE FIFTH SWORD OF SORROW: MARY STANDS AT THE FOOT OF THE CROSS (JOHN 19:25-27)

The Blessed Virgin Mary continued to climb the mount to Calvary, following behind Jesus painfully and sorrowfully, yet suffering silently. She could see Him staggering and falling with the cross some more, and she witnessed her Son being beaten by soldiers who pulled His hair to force Him to stand up. Despite His innocence, when Jesus reached the top of Calvary, He was ordered to confess in front of the crowd so they could laugh at Him. Mary deeply felt her Son's pain and humiliation, particularly when His tormentors forced Him to strip off what was left of His clothing. The Blessed Virgin felt sick at heart seeing these tyrants crucifying her Son naked, shaming Him terribly merely to amuse the jeering crowd. (Jesus and Mary felt more disgrace than normal people did because they were without sin and holy.)

The Blessed Virgin Mary felt pain beyond bearing when Jesus was stretched out on the Cross. His murderers sang merrily as they approached Him with hammers and nails. They sat on Him heavily so that He could not move when they spiked Him to the wood. As they hammered the nails through His hands and feet, Mary felt the blows in her heart; the nails pierced her flesh as they tore into her Son's body. She felt her life fading away.

As the soldiers lifted the Cross to drop it into the hole they had dug, they deliberately jerked it, causing the force of His body weight to tear through the flesh and expose His bone. The pain shot through His body like liquid fire.

Jesus endured three excruciating hours skewered on the Cross, yet the physical pain was nothing compared to the agonizing heartache He was forced to bear seeing His mother suffering below Him. Mercifully, He finally died.

Prayer: *Beloved Mother, Queen of the Martyrs, give us the courage you had in all your sufferings so that we may unite our sufferings with yours and give glory to God. Help us follow all His commandments and those of the Church so that Our Lord's sacrifice will not be in vain, and all sinners in the world will be saved.* ***(Pray 1 Our Father and 7 Hail Mary's)***

Most Merciful Mother, remind us always about the Sorrows of your Son, Jesus.

6. THE SIXTH SWORD OF SORROW: MARY RECEIVES THE DEAD BODY OF JESUS IN HER ARMS (JOHN 19:38-40)

Mary could see the terrifying wounds from the flogging Jesus had received while at Pilate's. His flesh had been shredded and large strips had been torn from His back. His entire body had been so lacerated that gaping wounds crisscrossed Him from head to toe. Mary found that the wounds from the nails were less severe than those caused by the flogging and by carrying the Cross. She was horrified at the thought that her Son had managed to carry the heavy, splintered Cross all the way to Calvary. She saw the circle of blood the Crown of Thorns had made on His forehead and, to her horror, realized that many of the barbed thorns had dug so deeply into His skull they had penetrated His brain. Looking at her broken Boy, the Holy Mother knew that His agonizing death was far worse than the torture reserved for the wickedest of criminals.

As she cleaned His damaged Body she envisioned Him during each stage of His short life, remembering her first look at His beautiful new born face as they lay in the manger, and every day in between, until this heart rending moment as she gently bathed His lifeless Body. Her anguish was relentless as she prepared her Son and Lord for burial, but she remained brave and strong, becoming the true Queen of Martyrs. As she washed her Son she prayed that everybody would know the riches of Paradise and enter the Gates of Heaven. She prayed for every soul in the world to embrace God's Love, so her Son's torturous death would benefit all humankind and not have been in vain. Mary prayed for the world; she prayed for all of us.

Prayer: *We thank you, Beloved Mother, for your courage as you stood beneath your dying Child to comfort Him on the Cross. As our Savior drew His last breath, you became a wonderful Mother to all of us; you became the Blessed Mother of the world. We know that you love us more than our own earthly parents do. We implore you to be our advocate before the Throne of Mercy and Grace so that we can truly become your children. We thank you for Jesus, our Savior and Redeemer, and we thank Jesus for giving you to us. Please pray for us, Mother.*

(Pray 1 Our Father and 7 Hail Mary's)

Most Merciful Mother, remind us always about the Sorrows of your Son, Jesus.

7. THE SEVENTH SWORD OF SORROW: THE BODY OF JESUS IS PLACED IN THE TOMB (JOHN 19:41-42)

The life of the Blessed Virgin Mary was so closely linked to that of Jesus she thought there was no reason for her to go on living any longer. Her only comfort was that His death had ended His unspeakable suffering. Our Sorrowful Mother, with the help of John and the Holy women, devoutly placed the Body in the sepulcher, and she left Him. She went home with great pain and tremendous Sorrow; for the first time she was without Him, and her loneliness was a new and bitter source of pain. Her heart had been dying since her Son's heart had stopped beating, but she was certain that our Savior would soon be resurrected.

Prayer: *Most Beloved Mother, whose beauty surpasses that of all mothers, Mother of Mercy, Mother of Jesus, and Mother to us all, we are your children and we place all our trust in you. Teach us to see God in all things and all situations, even our sufferings. Help us to understand the importance of suffering, and also to know the purpose of our suffering as God had intended it.*

You yourself were conceived and born without sin, were preserved from sin, yet you suffered more than anybody else. You accepted suffering and pain with love and with unsurpassed courage. You stood by your

Son from the time He was arrested until He died. You suffered along with Him, felt His every pain and torment. You accomplished the Will of God the Father; and according to His will, you have become our Mother. We beg you, dear Mother, to teach us to do as Jesus did. Teach us to accept our cross courageously. We trust you, most Merciful Mother, so teach us to sacrifice for all the sinners in the world. Help us to follow in your Son's footsteps, and even to be willing to lay down our lives for others. **(Pray 1 Our Father and 7 Hail Mary's)**

Most Merciful Mother, remind us always about the Sorrows of your Son, Jesus.

Concluding Prayer: Queen of Martyrs, your heart suffered so much. I beg you, by the merits of the tears you shed in these terrible and sorrowful times, to obtain for me and all the sinners of the world the grace of complete sincerity and repentance. Amen.

Three times, say: Mary, who was conceived without sin and who suffered for us, pray for us.

Sign of the Cross: In the name of The Father, and The Son, and The Holy Spirit. Amen.

(Source: https://www.immaculee.com)

Litany of Our Lady
of Sorrows

Lord, have mercy on us.

Christ, have mercy on us.

Lord, have mercy on us.

Christ, hear us.

Christ, graciously hear us.

God the Father of heaven, have mercy on us.

God the Son, Redeemer of the world, have mercy on us.

God the Holy Spirit, have mercy on us.

Holy Trinity, one God, have mercy on us.

Holy Mary, pray for us.

Holy Mother of God, pray for us.

Holy Virgin of virgins, pray for us.

Mother of the Crucified, pray for us.

Sorrowful Mother, pray for us.

Mournful Mother, pray for us.

Sighing Mother, pray for us.

Afflicted Mother, pray for us.

Desolate Mother, pray for us.

Mother most sad, pray for us.

Mother set around with anguish, pray for us.

Mother overwhelmed by grief, pray for us.

Mother transfixed by a sword, pray for us.

Mother crucified in thy heart, pray for us.

Mother bereaved of thy Son, pray for us.

Sighing Dove, pray for us.
Mother of Dolors, pray for us.
Fount of tears, pray for us.
Sea of bitterness, pray for us.
Field of tribulation, pray for us.
Mass of suffering, pray for us.
Mirror of patience, pray for us.
Rock of constancy, pray for us.
Remedy in perplexity, pray for us.
Joy of the afflicted, pray for us.
Ark of the desolate, pray for us.
Refuge of the abandoned, pray for us.
Shield of the oppressed, pray for us.
Conqueror of the incredulous, pray for us.
Solace of the wretched, pray for us.
Medicine of the sick, pray for us.
Help of the faint, pray for us.
Strength of the weak, pray for us.
Protectress of those who fight, pray for us.
Haven of the shipwrecked, pray for us.
Calmer of tempests, pray for us.
Companion of the sorrowful, pray for us.
Retreat of those who groan, pray for us.
Terror of the treacherous, pray for us.
Standard-bearer of the martyrs, pray for us.
Treasure of the faithful, pray for us.
Light of confessors, pray for us.
Pearl of virgins, pray for us.

Comfort of widows, pray for us.

Joy of all saints, pray for us.

Queen of thy servants, pray for us.

Holy Mary, who alone art unexampled, pray for us.

Pray for us, most Sorrowful Virgin, that we may be made worthy of the promises of Christ.

Let us pray: O God, in whose Passion, according to the prophecy of Simeon, a sword of grief pierced through the most sweet soul of Thy glorious Blessed Virgin Mother Mary: grant that we, who celebrate the memory of her Seven Sorrows, may obtain the happy effect of Thy Passion, who lives and reigns world without end. Amen. (Pope Pius VII)

CHAPTER 5 - THE PRECIOUS BLOOD DEVOTION AND SEER BARNABAS OF NIGERIA

O f all the places chosen by Heaven to plant a seed of holiness where the Church's final victory would commence, Nigeria was chosen. Since July 1995 to the present, Our Lord Jesus Christ has been appearing to a university student called Barnabas Nwoye from Olo, Enugu State, Nigeria. Through this visionary, Our Lord has introduced the final weapon for all His children to endure and overcome the Great Chastisement, THE PRECIOUS BLOOD DEVOTION!

The messages of 1997 – 2000 received by seer Barnabas were reviewed by a Theological

Commission set up by Bishop Anthony Gbuji of Enugu State. They have received the Nihil Obstat of Rev. Fr. Stephen Obiukwu, Chairman of the Propagation of the Faith.

Messages To Seer Barnabas

"My child, listen. I have warned My people that the hour to save is short and that the days are numbered.

You have seen what will happen to My children who trust in Me, My faithful children.

That is why I came and gave you My Holy Chaplet of My Precious Blood and promised to save through My Precious Blood. I promise to also save any sinner who calls on My Precious Blood.

I will allow a drop of the Precious Blood to fall on their hearts so that they will get converted before the day of forsaking..."

Jesus Christ, 16th January 1997, after showing Barnabas a fearful vision of the torture of The Remnant by the Antichrist.

"My son, I tell you only one fourth of My Priests will be left after the Great Chastisement... My son, pray your Holy Rosary always as My Mother has ordered you

.

Pray the Holy Chaplet of My Precious Blood immediately after your Rosary. You must do this because the hour of salvation is short."

Jesus Christ, 19th January 1997, after showing Barnabas the final massacre of Priests.

"My children, this Chaplet of the Precious Blood of My Son combines all the devotions of My Son's Passion.

In Heaven, this prayer is one of the greatest prayers

that ceases the anger of the Eternal Father and bring mercy to the world."

Our Blessed Mother, 29th January 1997

To Those Who Pray
the Chaplet

1. I promise to protect any person who devoutly prays this Chaplet against evil attacks.
2. I will guard his five senses.
3. I will protect him from sudden death.
4. Twelve hours before his death, he will drink
   My Precious Blood and eat My Body.
5. Twenty-four hours before his death, I will show him my five wounds that he may feel a deep contrition for all his sins and have a perfect knowledge of them.
6. Any person who makes a novena with it will get their intentions. His prayer will be answered.
7. I will perform many wonderful miracles through it.
8. Through it, I will destroy many secret societies and set free many souls in bondage, by My mercy.
9. Through it, I will save many souls from Purgatory.
10. I will teach him My way, he who honors My Precious Blood through this Chaplet.
11. I will have mercy on them who have mercy on My Precious Wounds and Blood.

12. Whoever teaches this prayer to another person will have an indulgence of four years.

Prayers of the Chaplet of the Precious Blood

Opening: Hymn Most Precious Blood of Jesus Christ
Most Precious Blood of Jesus Christ
Most Precious Blood of Jesus Christ
Most Precious Blood of Jesus Christ
Most Precious Blood, save the world.

Invocation of the Holy Spirit
Come, Holy Spirit, fill the hearts of Your faithful and kindle in them the fire of Your love.
L: Send forth Your Spirit and they shall be created.
R: And You shall renew the face of the earth.

Let us Pray,

O God, Who did teach the hearts of the faithful by the light of the Holy Spirit, grant us by the same Spirit to be truly wise and ever rejoice in His consolations, through Christ Our Lord. Amen.

Apostles Creed ...
(Bow Your Head)

May the Precious Blood that pours out from the Sacred Head of Our Lord Jesus Christ, the Temple of Divine Wisdom, Tabernacle of Divine Knowledge and Sunshine of heaven and earth, cover us now and forever. Amen.

L: O most Precious Blood of Jesus Christ.
R: Heal the wounds in the most Sacred Heart of Jesus.

Our Father ... 3 Hail Mary's ... Glory Be ...
(Bow Your Head)
May the Precious Blood that pours out from the Sacred Head of Our Lord Jesus Christ, the Temple of Divine Wisdom, Tabernacle of Divine Knowledge and Sunshine of heaven and earth, cover us now and forever. Amen.

THE FIRST MYSTERY

The Nailing of the Right Hand of Our Lord Jesus
(Pause for brief meditation)
By the precious wound in Your right hand and through the pain of the nail which pierced Your right hand, may the Precious Blood that pours out from there save sinners of the whole world and convert many souls. Amen.

L: O most Precious Blood of Jesus Christ
R: Heal the wounds in the most Sacred Heart of Jesus.

Our Father ... Hail Mary ...
L: Precious Blood of Jesus Christ

R: Save us and the whole world. (12 times)

Glory Be ...
(Bow Your Head)
May the Precious Blood that pours out from the Sacred Head of Our Lord Jesus Christ, the Temple of Divine Wisdom, Tabernacle of Divine Knowledge and Sunshine of heaven and earth, cover us now and forever. Amen.

THE SECOND MYSTERY

The Nailing of the Left Hand of Our Lord Jesus
(Pause for brief meditation)
By the precious wound in Your left hand and through the pain of the nail which pierced Your left hand, may the Precious Blood that pours out from there save souls in Purgatory and protect the dying against the attack of infernal spirits. Amen.
L: O most Precious Blood of Jesus Christ
R: Heal the wounds in the most Sacred Heart of Jesus

Our Father ... Hail Mary ...
L: Precious Blood of Jesus Christ
R: Save us and the whole world. (12 times)

Glory Be ...
(Bow Your Head)
May the Precious Blood that pours out from the Sacred Head of Our Lord Jesus Christ, the Temple of Divine Wisdom, Tabernacle of Divine Knowledge

and Sunshine of heaven and earth, cover us now and forever. Amen.

THE THIRD MYSTERY

The Nailing of the Right Foot of
Our Lord Jesus
(Pause for brief meditation)
By the precious wound in Your right foot and through the pain of the nail which pierced Your right foot, may the Precious Blood that pours out from there cover the foundation of the Catholic Church against the plans of the occult kingdom and evil men. Amen.

L: O most Precious Blood of Jesus Christ
R: Heal the wounds in the most Sacred Heart of Jesus.
Our Father ... Hail Mary ...

L: Precious Blood of Jesus Christ
R: Save us and the whole world. (12 times)
Glory Be ...
(Bow Your Head)
May the Precious Blood that pours out from the Sacred Head of Our Lord Jesus Christ, the Temple of Divine Wisdom, Tabernacle of Divine Knowledge and Sunshine of heaven and earth, cover us now and forever. Amen.

THE FOURTH MYSTERY

The Nailing of the Left Foot of Our Lord Jesus
(Pause for brief meditation)

By the precious wound in Your left foot, and through the pain of the nail which pierced Your left foot, may the Precious Blood that pours out from there protect us in all our ways against the plans and the attacks of evil spirits and their agents. Amen.

L: O most Precious Blood of Jesus Christ
R: Heal the wounds in the most Sacred Heart of Jesus.

Our Father ... Hail Mary ...

L: Precious Blood of Jesus Christ
R: Save us and the whole world. (12 times)

Glory Be ...
(Bow Your Head)

May the Precious Blood that pours out from the Sacred Head of Our Lord Jesus Christ, the Temple of Divine Wisdom, Tabernacle of Divine Knowledge and Sunshine of heaven and earth, cover us now and forever. Amen.

THE FIFTH MYSTERY

The Piercing of the Sacred Side of
Our Lord Jesus
(Pause for brief meditation)
By the precious wound in Your Sacred Side and
through the pain of the lance which pierced Your
Sacred Side, may the Precious Blood and water that
pour out from there cure the sick, raise the dead,
solve our present problems and teach us the way to
our God for eternal glory. Amen.

L: O most Precious Blood of Jesus Christ
R: Heal the wounds in the most Sacred Heart of
Jesus.

Our Father ... Hail Mary ...

L: Precious Blood of Jesus Christ
R: Save us and the whole world. (12 times)

Glory Be ...
(Bow Your Head)
May the Precious Blood that pours out from the
Sacred Head of Our Lord Jesus Christ, the Temple
of Divine Wisdom, Tabernacle of Divine Knowledge
and Sunshine of heaven and earth, cover us now
and forever. Amen.

L: O most Precious Blood of Jesus Christ
R: Heal the wounds in the most Sacred Heart of
Jesus. (repeat 3 times)

Hail Holy Queen ...

Let us Pray

O most Precious Blood of Jesus Christ, we honor, worship and adore You because of Your work of the everlasting covenant that brings peace to mankind. Heal the wounds in the most Sacred Heart of Jesus. Console the Almighty Father on His throne and wash away the sins of the whole world. May all revere You, O Precious Blood, have mercy. Amen.

(Image from the Sisters of the Precious Blood)

THE LITANY OF THE MOST PRECIOUS BLOOD OF JESUS

L: Lord, have mercy on us
R: Lord, have mercy on us
L: Christ, have mercy on us
R: Christ, have mercy on us
L: Lord, have mercy on us
R: Lord, have mercy on us
L: Christ, hear us
R: Christ, graciously hear us

L: God, the Father of heaven
R: *have mercy on us
L: God the Son, Redeemer of the world *
L: God, the Holy Spirit *
L: Holy Trinity, One God *

L: O most Precious Blood of Jesus Christ, the Blood of Salvation
R: Cover us and the whole world.

L: The ocean of the Blood of Jesus Christ
R: Set us free
L: The Blood of Jesus Christ, Full of holiness and compassion

R: Set us free

L: Precious Blood of Jesus Christ, Our strength

and power

R: Set us free

L: Precious Blood of Jesus Christ,
The Everlasting Covenant

R: Set us free

L: Precious Blood of Jesus Christ,
The foundation of the Christian faith

R: Set us free

L: Precious Blood of Jesus Christ,
The armor of God

R: Set us free

L: Precious Blood of Jesus Christ,
The Divine Charity

R: Set us free

L: Precious Blood of Jesus Christ,
The scourge of demons

R: Set us free

L:Precious Blood of Jesus Christ,
The help of those in bondage

R: Set us free

L:Precious Blood of Jesus Christ,

The sacred wine

R: Set us free

L:Precious Blood of Jesus Christ,
The power of Christians

R: Set us free

L:Precious Blood of Jesus Christ,
The defender of the Catholic wall

R: Set us free

L:Precious Blood of Jesus Christ,
The Christian's true faith

R: Set us free

L:Precious Blood of Jesus Christ,
The healing blood

R: Save Us

L:Precious Blood of Jesus Christ,
The anointing blood

R: Save Us

L:Precious Blood of Jesus Christ,
The boldness of the children of God

R: Save Us

L:Precious Blood of Jesus Christ,

The commander of Christian warriors

R: Save Us

L:Precious Blood of Jesus Christ,
The blood of resurrection

R: Save Us

L:Precious Blood of Jesus Christ,
The drink of heavenly angels

R: Save Us

L:Precious Blood of Jesus Christ,
The consolation of God the Father

R: Save Us

L:Precious Blood of Jesus Christ,
The power of the Holy Spirit

R: Save Us

L:Precious Blood of Jesus Christ,
The circumcision of the Gentiles

R: Save Us

L:Precious Blood of Jesus Christ,
The peace of the world

R: Save Us

L:Precious Blood of Jesus Christ,

The sunshine of heaven and earth

R: Save Us

L:Precious Blood of Jesus Christ,
The rainbow in heaven

R: Save Us

L:Precious Blood of Jesus Christ,
The hope of innocent children

R: Save Us

L:Precious Blood of Jesus Christ,

The Word of God in our hearts

R: Save Us

L:Precious Blood of Jesus Christ,

The heavenly weapon

R: Save Us

L: Precious Blood of Jesus Christ,

The Divine Wisdom

R: Save Us

L:Precious Blood of Jesus Christ,

The foundation of the world

R: Save Us

L: Precious Blood of Jesus Christ,

The mercy of God the Father

R: Save Us

L: O most Precious Blood of Jesus Christ
R: Cleanse the sins of the world

L: O most Precious Blood of Jesus Christ
R: Refine the world
L: O most Precious Blood of Jesus Christ
R: Teach us how to console Jesus

Let us Pray
O Precious Blood of our salvation, we believe, hope and trust in You. Deliver all those that are in the hands of the infernal spirits we beseech You. Protect the dying against the works of evil spirits and welcome them into Your eternal glory. Have mercy on the whole world and strengthen us to worship and console the Sacred Heart. We adore you, O Precious Blood of mercy. Amen.

L: O most Precious Blood of Jesus Christ
R: Heal the wounds in the most Sacred Heart of Jesus. (repeat 3 times)

Hymn
Blood of Jesus

Blood of Jesus
Blood of Jesus, cover us (3 times)

Prayers of Adoration of the Blood of Jesus

Adoration Precious Blood of Jesus
Adoration Precious Blood of Jesus Christ

We adore You Precious Blood of Jesus
We adore You Precious Blood of Jesus Christ

Adoration Precious Blood of Jesus
Adoration Precious Blood of Jesus Christ

The Agonizing Crucifix

On the 5th January 2000, Barnabas witnessed a vision of Jesus walking alone in a desert. The visionary relates that as Jesus came closer, He held up a crucifix to Barnabas saying,

"Barnabas, take this."

After handing the crucifix over, Jesus continued,

"This is your crucified Lord who loves you. He is the one whom you daily crucify.

Accept it from Me, carry it always. Show it the world; let all men have it also. Children, this is what your sins do to Me."

The visionary taking the crucifix closer, observed that the difference was that the wounds and scourges of our Lord's body appeared well. Blood oozed continuously from it.

On the crucifix was written the inscription:

'I am the Agonizing Jesus Christ who loves you.'

To Those Who Devotedly Venerate The Agonizing Crucifix

1. To prepare you for the battle, I give you My Agonizing Crucifix. I promise to protect anyone who has this Crucifix against the evil forces.

2. Through this Crucifix, I will deliver many from captivity.

3. Whenever you raise this Crucifix against evil power, I will open heaven and let My Precious Blood flow to subdue the evil power.

4. I will let My Precious Blood flow from all My Sacred Wounds and cover all who venerate My Wounds and Blood through this Crucifix.

5. I promise to protect any house where this Crucifix is against any destructive power in the hour of darkness.

6. I promise to perform numerous miracles through this Crucifix.

7. I will break their hearts of stone and pour My love on them that venerate My Agonizing Crucifix.

8. I promise also to draw straying souls closer to Myself through this Crucifix.

9. Children, in the days of the evil one you will be able to go freely without any harm through this Crucifix.

Finally, Our Lord emphasized; "Children, through

this Cross I will conquer. This Cross will soon be a victorious Cross."
(Source:www.preciousbloodinternational.com)

CONSECRATION TO
THE PRECIOUS BLOOD
OF JESUS CHRIST

Conscious, merciful Savior, of my nothingness and of Thy sublimity, I cast myself at Thy feet and thank Thee for the many proofs of Thy grace shown unto me, Thy ungrateful creature. I thank Thee especially for delivering me by Thy Precious Blood from the destructive power of Satan. In the presence of my dear Mother Mary, my guardian angel, my patron saint, and of the whole company of heaven, I dedicate myself voluntarily with a sincere heart, O dearest Jesus, to Thy Precious Blood, by which Thou hast redeemed the world from sin, death and hell. I promise Thee, with the help of Thy grace and to the utmost of my strength to stir up and foster devotion to Thy Precious Blood, the price of our redemption, so that Thy adorable Blood may be honored and glorified by all. In this way, I wish to make reparation for my disloyalty towards Thy Precious Blood of love, and to make satisfaction to Thee for the many profanations which men commit against that precious price of their salvation. O would that my own sins, my coldness, and all the acts of disrespect I have ever committed against Thee, O Holy Precious Blood, could be undone. Behold, O dearest Jesus, I offer to Thee the love, honor and adoration, which Thy most Holy Mother, Thy faithful disciples and all the saints have offered to Thy Precious Blood. I ask Thee to forget my earlier faithlessness and coldness, and to forgive all who offend Thee. Sprinkle me, O Divine Savior, and all men with Thy Precious Blood, so that we, O Crucified Love, may love Thee from now on with all our hearts, and worthily honor the price of our salvation. Amen.

We fly to thy patronage, O holy Mother of God; despise not our petitions in our necessities, but deliver us always from all dangers, O glorious and blessed Virgin. Amen.

(Miraculous Agonising Jesus Christ Crucifix Oozing Blood)

CHAPTER 6 - THE QUEEN AND MOTHER OF THE END TIMES WITH SEER LUZ DE MARIA

DESCRIPTION OF THE IMAGE

I share with you the description that our Blessed Mother explained to me about the symbols that make up the image of this invocation:

"Upon My image rests the Holy Spirit, of whom I am Temple and Tabernacle.

My Crown has three Crosses: the middle Cross belongs to My Son's Cross, the one on the right to remind you of Divine Mercy and how the repentant thief attained forgiveness and won Heaven, and the one on the left for you to keep in mind the one who mocked My Son, being on a cross, and condemned himself.

The Scapular on My Chest is a sign of the commitment that My children have so that their life be alike to Mine: in obedience and faith to the Word of God.

My Sacred Heart illuminates the life of men and, in the end, My Immaculate Heart will triumph.

In My Womb, My Son is seen in the Holy Eucharist, unfolding His Love through yellow rays.

On the wrists of My Hands you will notice a star, so that you remember that I am the Morning Star of the New Dawn and guide the People of My Son.

My Hands shine with light so that My children do not go astray and see the light of the beacon of My Hands, from which rays emanate that converge with the rays of My Son, present in the Holy Eucharist and deposit themselves in blessing on the newborn child, who represents, in the first place, Our beloved Angel of Peace—fruit of the Trinitarian Will—who is presented to Humanity by the Hand of God the Father who is guarding him. Second, the child represents the Holy Remnant. That Holy Remnant that is being protected and maintained on the Earth of peace, by the Hand of God the Almighty Father.

The Earth, at this instant, is surrounded by My Holy Rosary, just as the renewed Earth will continue to be surrounded by My Holy Rosary. And with each Our Father and every Hail Mary that you have prayed in the Rosaries and in other prayers, you have multiplied them to infinity, because prayers will always bear fruits of life and in abundance.

The Earth is shining, and the darkness will have passed.

My Invocation represents the Hope of a new Heaven and a new earth.

Amen."

✝ IMPRIMATUR,
Bishop of Diocese of Estelí

The Queen and Mother
of the End Times

The Blessed Virgin Mary was revealed to Luz de María by our Lord Jesus Christ **under the title of "QUEEN AND MOTHER OF THE END TIMES"**.

Later the Heavenly Mother dictated a prayer for all of God's People, with which She invites us to invoke Her especially in these instants of great tribulation and confusion inside and outside the Church.

Grateful to Heaven for such a great heavenly gift, we exhort the People of God to receive with faith and gratitude over this divine help that springs from the loving Will of God that wants to protect all of us in the present and the future through the maternal help of the "Queen and Mother of the End Times".

CONSECRATION TO THE
QUEEN AND MOTHER
OF THE END TIMES

Dictated by the Blessed Virgin Mary to Luz de Maria in the Year of the Lord, August 28, 2021

Queen and Mother of the End Times,
Today I consecrate myself to You and with me I

consecrate all my family and friends
and I beg you to protect those who feel they are my
enemies.

I freely wish to ask you to always intercede
before the Trinitarian Throne to save my soul.

I beg You Mother to live in me
so I can be worthy of Your Son
until I am called into His Presence.

You know that we must expand the kingdom of
your Son,
Queen and Mother of the End Times, Sacred Gift of
God,
refuge of those who in one voice pronounce:

Hail Mary most pure conceived without sin,
pray for the banished from this life.

I firmly believe in Your Maternal Protection,
in the time when I feel shaken.

You are health to the sick,
today I ask you to heal the sick of body and spirit
so that evil may be stopped.

You know the calamities of your Son's people,
before them today I give you my heart, soul, powers
and senses.
I want to be all yours and for You
to go towards Christ, my Lord and my God.

Amen.

NOVENA TO THE
QUEEN AND MOTHER
OF THE END TIMES

As a preparation to the Festivity of August 28th.

Start date: August 20th
End date: August 28th

The following Novena has been dictated to Luz de María by Our Blessed Mother. Each day of the Novena, Our Blessed Mother wishes that, united with Her, we say the initial prayer, the prayer of the day and lovingly carry out the offering that She indicates. In the same way, She also reminds us:

"As all My children know, during a Novena it is necessary to attend the Holy Eucharist."

Note: This Novena can be done with love and devotion at any time of the year.

PRAYER TO THE QUEEN AND MOTHER OF THE END TIMES

Beloved children, I invite you to pray:

Divine Father, Eternal and Omnipotent,
Holy Son, Word Incarnate,
Holy Paraclete, Divine Spirit,
Three Persons in one True God.

Pour out Your Most Holy Blessing upon this creature
who cries out before Your Divine Majesty.
Take my hand so that I am not separated from Your Protection,
give me the immovable hope
of the encounter with Your Glory.

May my soul be sculpted by Your Holy Spirit
and I find the discernment
that leads me to the Truth of Your Word
and I do not deviate from the Holy Path.

Most Holy Trinity, you have bequeathed to Your People
the blessing of possessing
the Queen and Mother of the End Times,
to intercede for and defend Your People.

I welcome such an exalted Queen and Mother,
I take Her blessed Hand and I surrender to Her Maternal Instruction
so that, together with Her, I may be a doer of Your Will.

Mother who guides, Mother who intercedes,
Mother who protects this aimless Humanity,
be my helm at this instant,so that, before the clutches of evil,
my soul does not succumb out of weakness.
Give me the willpower so that I may not fear the

waiting,
But rather that I may fear falling into the insinuations of evil
and do not let my soul be lost in the darkness of evil.

Queen and Mother of the End Times,
come, receive me and teach me
to wait for the Trinitarian instant,
may it not be I who wishes to advance the hour,
but under the protection of Your faithfulness,
may I be Your reflection and may no instant frighten me before which it looks like I may succumb.

Queen and Mother of the End Times,
Make Love, Faith, and Hope, be reborn in me
and also, the courage to live like You,
nourishing myself with the Trinitarian Will
and continuing with the fervent faith that You will lead me
towards the longed-for encounter with the Father, the Son and the Holy Spirit, being reborn to the new life beside the Most Sacrosanct Trinity. Amen.

FIRST DAY

Pray for the conversion of Humanity.

Prayer of the day:

Queen and Mother look at me, I live alone,
come to me, I need Your Love.
Place my petitions in Your Heart,
which I beg you to accept: (add personal petitions here).
Illuminate me with the rays of Your Obedience,
Faith, Hope and Charity.
I wish to help my brothers and sisters with Your same Obedience,
so that together, we may know Your beloved Son.
Amen.

Offering: I invite you to offer My Son obedience.

SECOND DAY

Pray for those who do not know the Most Holy Trinity.

Prayer to the Queen and Mother of the End Times...
Prayer of the day:

May Your Heart be the treasure where I discover the infinite dimension of Trinitarian Love.
Do not let me be an ungrateful child who denies the Creator,
do not let me be a blind creature who denies

Redemption,
do not let me be so deluded as to think that without
the Holy Spirit, my conscience can be enlightened
to discern between
what is of God and what is not of God.

Queen and Mother, I beg You that I may be
an instrument for the good of my brothers and
sisters. Amen.

Offering: On this day I ask you to carry out works
of mercy towards the needy.

THIRD DAY

**Pray that the persecutors and enemies of My Son's
People will be dispersed.**

**Prayer to the Queen and Mother of the End
Times...**
Prayer of the day:

Queen and Mother of the weighed down,
look for me, I call You with all my strength.
Do not allow my reason be greater than my heart,
ignite in me the courage to take the path of
conversion.

Even if I be persecuted on Earth for loving Your
Son,
bring Your Angels and come with me,
come and teach me to resist by looking,
at every moment, Your Motherly Face,
may Your gaze penetrate my thoughts,
and may I not drift away no matter how much

the world offers me the fruits that would lead me to sin.

Receive, Queen and Mother, my wishes
and in You, make them come true. Amen.

Offering: I call you to adore My Son.

FOURTH DAY
Offer this day for your personal conversion.

Prayer to the Queen and Mother of the End Times ...
Prayer of the day:

May the joy of looking at You lead me to continue delivering the best of me each and every day.
I offer myself, so You can polish me, I do not want to be lost,
evil confuses me and the mundane overwhelms me,
I am going through difficult moments, my humanity falters...

Queen and Mother fill my heart with Your Strength
and my mind with Your Obedience and Firmness.
I want to go forward towards Eternal Life,
I yearn for my human ego to be an instrument
for spiritual growth.

Queen and Mother fill me with Your Gifts,
help me to overcome the need
of wanting to always be the best and the most applauded.

Come, Queen of Heaven and Mother of Your Son's People,
make me a new person,
innocent, that surrenders at Your feet
to grow under the protection of Your Purity. Amen.

Offering: Share food with the needy.

FIFTH DAY
This day I call you to love your brothers and sisters and not to reject them.

Prayer to the Queen and Mother of the End Times ...

Prayer of the day:

My Jesus, teach me to look at Your Face in my fellow men,
I need my eyes not to be so human,
I need them to be more spiritual so,
they will see with Your same Love.

Queen and Mother share with me the light from Your Gaze
which You possess from the Holy Spirit.

Come, I beg of You, so that my mind, my thoughts
and my heart be more in the Divine way
so that pride, prejudices, and feeling saved and
more than my brothers and sisters be detached from me.

My Jesus, I want to be fully aware of what it is to be Your son
and a member of Your People.

Aware so that I not feel saved by saying that I love you,
instead, that I realize that he who loves You
loves his neighbor without distinctions. Amen.

Offering: I ask you offer Holy Communion for your brothers and sisters, those you do not love as you should.

SIXTH DAY

On this day, you will bless all the brothers and sisters that you see; you will bless them all with your mind, with your thoughts and with your heart: all of them.

Prayer to the Queen and Mother of the End Times...

Prayer of the day:

Queen and Mother of the End Times,
come and take my mind, my thoughts and my heart,
so that it be You who blesses my brothers and sisters in me.

As I am incapable of blessing without distinctions and
not having fulfilled the First Commandment,
I pray for Your Motherly help,
that I be obedient to the Commandment of Love.

Queen and Mother, come and renew my heart so I may love my brothers and sisters as Your Son loves:
without distinctions.

Give me a renewed mind and thoughts
not to create obstacles in my heart that interfere,
thereby denying myself Eternal Salvation. Amen.

Offering: On this day you will resolve to be love
to your fellow men so that jealousy, envy, vanity,
desire for possession, lack of love, and materialism
disappear.

SEVENTH DAY
Offer this day so that fidelity grows, and you do
not wane during the serious instants.

**Prayer to the Queen and Mother of the End
Times ...**
Prayer:

Loving Father, Merciful Son, Holy Spirit, the
comforter,
Be adored everywhere.
Omnipotent and Everlasting God,
send Your Holy Spirit upon me,
I prostrate myself before Your Majesty,
I humbly implore for the Gift of Fortitude
that I do not decline no matter how strong the
trials may be.
Most Holy Trinity, I abandon myself in You
so that I awaken in this instant
and my vision not be clouded by modernisms.
Give me strength to remain faithful to Your
Word
and to be compliant of Your Commandments,

convinced that this is the good for
my salvation and that of my fellow men.

Give me Holy Wisdom to understand that
in order to love you, I must deepen my knowledge
and understanding of Your Word.

Queen and Mother of the End Times,
I come to Your Shelter so that You be the beacon
that illuminates my path. Amen.

Offering: Children, on this day you will meditate
on how far away man is from God.

EIGHTH DAY
**Make reparation for the distance of man towards
his Creator and the unbelief towards His Word.**

**Prayer to the Queen and Mother of the End
Times...**

Prayer:

Queen of my life, come, take my physical senses
and lead them to recognize the evil that exits
in all that surrounds us,
so that my senses will not lead me to what is
improper.

I offer you my human will,
keep it in Your Hands and hold it,
so that I will not be indifferent
to the Divine Love nor to my neighbor.

I surrender to Your Maternal Guidance,
as Your child who does not want to take
the wrong path and lose Salvation. Amen.

Offering: On this day, you will do an act of mercy.

NINTH DAY
I call you to consecrate yourselves.

Prayer to the Queen and Mother of the End Times ...

Consecration Prayer

Queen and Mother of the End Times,
I am your child, receive me, I give to You my life
and in Your Hands, I place my will,
all I have and all I am, my aspirations, desires and projects.

Take away from me all attachment to material things,
so that I will look for possessions
which cannot be seen because they are spiritual.

I consecrate my life to You today, Queen and Mother,
I freely surrender to Your Protection
in such difficult instants in which I live,
be the Ark that will lead me to remain afloat
without sinking in the middle of the purification.

May the Rays from Your Hands enlighten my mind,
my thoughts and my memories that they be healed,
my sufferings, so that I offer it and my falls,
so that You will lift me.
Illuminate my reason so that it does not compete with my faith,
but one be the light of the other.

I consecrate myself to You and surrender to You within the freedom of the God´s children. Amen.

AFTER DOING THIS NOVENA YOU WILL RECEIVE FROM ME:

† The virtue of Hope, so that you do not desist in the instants when you feel the path seems long, and so that the happiness of being a child of God will not move away.

† I will not allow despair to take hold of you, neither will allow you to believe that My Son has abandoned you. Whoever asks for mercy of heart and firm purpose of amendment will receive them.

† I will provide you with the Gift of Wisdom, so you will be children attached to the Divine Word and not be confused, as children who look the Mission that God has entrusted to them. In this way you will not harm the Divine Plans.

† You will receive the Gift of Strength so that your faith will be firm and strong, persevering, and at the same time, love guides all.

† Families will be more united and fraternity among brothers and sisters will be stopper to evil.

† I will provide love between spouses so that it increases.

MY BLESSING WILL BE WITH YOU AS LONG AS YOU ACT WITHIN WHAT IS GOOD. I love you.
(Source: https://www.revelacionesmarianas.com)

THE PROPHETIC MESSAGE OF GUADALUPE - The Woman Clothed With The Sun With The Moon Under Her Feet

This great prodigy that Our Blessed Mother propitiated that 12th December of 1531, capturing Herself in the Tilma as "Our Lady of Guadalupe" is one of the great signs for this generation, through which Heaven invites mankind to look beyond ourselves, motivating us to a transcendental search in our destiny as children of God in the infinity of creation and **revealing, at the same time, a universal event reserved for the end of this generation.** According to the messages given to Luz de María by Our Lord Jesus Christ and the Blessed Virgin is that we consider observing in a special way this prodigy, since a great mystery to be unveiled is at the doors of this generation. A prophecy of hope, implicit in the image of the tilma, which we interpret as a great help that Heaven will give to man in the most critical instant of the great tribulation.

OUR LORD JESUS CHRIST TO LUZ DE MARIA (12.11.2018)

MY PEOPLE, CELEBRATE THE WOMAN CLOTHED

WITH THE SUN WITH THE MOON UNDER HER FEET (cf. Apoc 12,1), THE WOMAN WHO REMAINS WITH CHILD THE HUMBLE AND SIMPLE TO REVEAL HERSELF. SUCH IS MY MOTHER, SHE USES WHAT THE WORLD DESPISES SO THAT THE WORK OF MY HOUSE MAY BE SEEN.

In this relationship of man with Creation this invocation of My Mother is that She tells the man of this generation, who has so many scientific advances at his disposal, *MARVEL AT THE WORK THAT BY DIVINE DECREE DWELLS WITHIN ME...! MY PEOPLE, WHAT BY DIVINE WILL REMAINS ON MY MOTHER'S TILMA IS YET TO BE REVEALED* and has not been found - but it will not be man who will unveil it, rather My House will unveil it to man.

(Miraculous Eyes of Our Lady of Guadalupe)

John Paul II's Prayer to
Our Lady of Guadalupe

O Immaculate Virgin, Mother of the true God and Mother of the Church!, who from this place reveal your clemency and your pity to all those who ask for your protection, hear the prayer that we address to you with filial trust, and present it to your Son Jesus, our sole Redeemer.

Mother of Mercy, Teacher of hidden and silent sacrifice, to you, who come to meet us sinners, we dedicate on this day all our being and all our love. We also dedicate to you our life, our work, our joys, our infirmities and our sorrows. Grant peace, justice and prosperity to our peoples; for we entrust to your care all that we have and all that we are, our Lady and Mother. We wish to be entirely yours and to walk with you along the way of complete faithfulness to Jesus Christ in His Church; hold us always with your loving hand.

Virgin of Guadalupe, Mother of the Americas, we pray to you for all the Bishops, that they may lead the faithful along paths of intense Christian life, of love and humble service of God and souls. Contemplate this immense harvest, and intercede with the Lord that He may instill a hunger for holiness in the whole people of God, and grant abundant vocations of priests and religious, strong in the faith and zealous dispensers of God's mysteries.

Grant to our homes the grace of loving and respecting life in its beginnings, with the same love with which you conceived in your womb the life of the Son of God. Blessed Virgin Mary, protect our families, so that they may always be united, and bless the upbringing of our children.

Our hope, look upon us with compassion, teach us to go continually to Jesus and, if we fall, help us to rise again, to return to Him, by means of the confession of our faults and sins in the Sacrament of Penance, which gives peace to the soul.

We beg you to grant us a great love for all the holy Sacraments, which are, as it were, the signs that your Son left us on earth. Thus, Most Holy Mother, with the peace of God in our conscience, with our hearts free from evil and hatred, we will be able to bring to all true joy and true peace, which come to us from your son, our Lord Jesus Christ, who with God the Father and the Holy Spirit, lives and reigns for ever and ever. Amen.

Original Image of Our Lady of Guadalupe

CHAPTER 7-
CONSECRATION OF
HOME AS A REFUGE
WITH SEER FATHER
MICHEL RODRIGUE

The Holy Family is a sign after which every family must model itself. I insist that every family that receives this message should have a representation of the Holy Family in their home. It can be an icon or a statue of the Holy Family or a permanent manger in a central place in the home. The representation must be blessed and consecrated by a priest.

As the star, followed by the Wise Men, stopped over the manger, the chastisement from the sky will not hit the Christian families devoted to and protected by the Holy Family. The fire from the sky is a chastisement for the horrible crime of abortion and the culture of death, the sexual perversion, and the cupidity regarding the identity of man and woman. My children seek perverted sins more than eternal life. The increase of blasphemies and persecution of My just people offends Me. The arm of My justice will come now. They do not hear My Divine Mercy. I must now let many plagues happen in order to save the most people I can from the slavery of Satan.

Send this message to everyone. I have given St. Joseph, My representative to protect the Holy Family on Earth, the authority to protect the Church, which is the Body of Christ. He will be the protector during the trials of this time. The Immaculate Heart of My daughter, Mary, and the

Sacred Heart of My Beloved Son, Jesus, with the chaste and pure heart of St. Joseph, will be the shield of your home, your family, and your refuge during the events to come.

My words are My blessing over all of you. Whoever acts according to My will, will be safe. The powerful love of the Holy Family will be manifested to all.

I am your Father.

These words are Mine!"

(Message from God the Father to Fr. Michel, 30 October 2018)

"The Miraculous Image" of the Holy Family

This Holy Family Image comes from a photograph that a sister took during the consecration of the Mass. When she developed the picture, she saw before her this image of the Holy Family and the hands of a priest in the bottom left corner, holding up the Host.

EXORCISM BLESSING FOR OIL & SPRINKLING ON IMAGE
(Use 100% pure virgin olive oil)

To be said by a priest (or deacon when the sacramental is for private devotion). In the event that a priest will not use the rite below, Fr. Michel notes that a simple blessing will still suffice.

(Priest or deacon vests in surplice and purple stole)

P: Our help is in the Name of the Lord.

R: Who made heaven and earth.

P: O oil, creature of God, I exorcise you by God the Father (+) almighty, who made heaven and earth and sea, and all that they contain. Let the adversary's power, the devil's legions, and all of Satan's attacks and machinations be dispelled and driven far from this creature, oil. Let it bring health in body and mind to all who use it, in the name of God (+) the Father almighty, and of our Lord Jesus (+) Christ, His Son, and of the Holy (+) Spirit, as well as in the love of the same Jesus Christ our Lord, who is coming to judge both the living and the dead and the world by fire.

R: Amen.

P: O Lord hear my prayer.

R: And let my cry come unto thee.

P: May the Lord be with you.

R: And with your spirit.

P: Let us pray. Lord God almighty, before whom the hosts of angels stand in awe, and whose heavenly service we acknowledge; may it please You to regard favorably and to bless (+) and hallow (+) this creature, oil, which by Your power has been pressed from the juice of olives. You have ordained it for anointing the sick, so that, when they are made well, they may give thanks to You, the living and true God. Grant we pray, that those who will use this oil, which we are blessing (+) in Your Name, may be protected from every attack of the unclean spirit, and be delivered from all suffering, all infirmity, and all wiles of the enemy. Let it be a means of averting any kind of adversity from man, redeemed by the Precious Blood of Your Son, so that he may never again suffer the sting of the ancient serpent. Through Christ our Lord.

R: Amen. (Priest or deacon then sprinkles the oil with holy water)

**(Father Michel Rodrigue with a Blessed
Image of the Holy Family)**

How To Consecrate Your Home and Land as a Refuge

1. For Your Home or Apartment

The following consecration is done by the owner of the property with exorcised water and exorcised salt. You are to recite the following prayers, as quoted by Fr Michel Rodrigue:

"In the Name of the Father, and of the Son, and of the Holy Spirit, God the Father, through your Beloved Son, Jesus Christ, who shed his blood on the cross to save us, I consecrate my home to you. It is Yours. Use it as You will for the safety of your people. I consecrate my home to You, through the intercession of the Immaculate Heart of Mary, to be under the wings of the Holy Spirit for the time of purification."

Sprinkle the holy water in the four corners of your house, making a sign of the cross as you say: In the name of the Father, and of the Son, and of the Holy Spirit. Amen

2. For Your Land

Bless it in the same way using exorcised water and salt and say the same prayer. However, instead of the words "I consecrate my home", use the words, "I consecrate my land".

"When the salt mingles with the earth, it enters into the land and consecrates it. God knows the size of your property and its boundaries" (Fr Michel Rodrigue) (Source: https://www.countdowntothekingdom.com/)

(May you be under the wings of the Holy Spirit for the time of purification)

Entrustment to the Sacred Hearts

"Send this message to everyone. I have given St. Joseph, My representative, to protect the Holy Family on Earth, the authority to protect the Church, which is the Body of Christ. He will be the protector during the trials of this time."

As St. Joseph protected the Body of the Baby Jesus, he will protect the Lord's Body, the Church.

"The Immaculate Heart of My daughter, Mary, and the Sacred Heart of My Beloved Son, Jesus, with the chaste and pure heart of St. Joseph, will be the shield of your home, your family, and your refuge during the events to come."

(God the Father to Fr. Michel Rodrigue, October 30, 2018)

With this exhortation, let us consecrate ourselves and families to the Sacred Hearts:

Memorare to Saint Joseph
(Recommended by Fr
Michel Rodrigue)

Remember,
 O most chaste spouse of the Virgin Mary,
that never was it known that anyone who implored your help
and sought your intercession were left unassisted.
Full of confidence in your power
 I fly unto you and beg your protection.
Despise not O Guardian of the Redeemer my humble supplication,
but in your bounty, hear and answer me.
Amen!

Act of Consecration
to St. Joseph

O dearest St. Joseph, I consecrate myself to your honor and give myself to you, that you may always be my father, my protector and my guide in the way of salvation.

Obtain for me a greater purity of heart and fervent love of the interior life.

After your example may I do all my actions for the

greater glory of God, in union with the Divine Heart of Jesus and the Immaculate Heart of Mary.
O Blessed St. Joseph, pray for me, that I may share in the peace and joy of your holy death. Amen.

(St Joseph, Protector of the Universal Church)

A Solemn Act of Consecration to the Immaculate Heart of Mary

Author: Venerable Pope Pius XII

Most Holy Virgin Mary, tender Mother of men, to fulfill the desires of the Sacred Heart of Jesus and the request of the Vicar of Your Son on earth, we consecrate ourselves and our families to your Sorrowful and Immaculate Heart, O Queen of the Most Holy Rosary, and we recommend to You, all the people of our country and all the world.

Please accept our consecration, dearest Mother, and use us as You wish to accomplish Your designs in the world.

O Sorrowful and Immaculate Heart of Mary, Queen of the Most Holy Rosary, and Queen of the World, rule over us, together with the Sacred Heart of Jesus Christ, Our King. Save us from the spreading flood of modern paganism; kindle in our hearts and homes the love of purity, the practice of a virtuous life, an ardent zeal for souls, and a desire to pray the Rosary more faithfully.

We come with confidence to You, O Throne of Grace and Mother of Fair Love. Inflame us with the same Divine Fire which has inflamed Your own

Sorrowful and Immaculate Heart. Make our hearts and homes Your shrine, and through us, make the Heart of Jesus, together with your rule, triumph in every heart and home.

Amen.

Act of Consecration to
the Sacred Heart

Author: St. Margaret Mary Alacoque

O Sacred Heart of Jesus, to Thee I consecrate and offer up my person and my life, my actions, trials, and sufferings, that my entire being may henceforth only be employed in loving, honoring and glorifying Thee. This is my irrevocable will, to belong entirely to Thee, and to do all for Thy love, renouncing with my whole heart all that can displease Thee.

I take Thee, O Sacred Heart, for the sole object of my love, the protection of my life, the pledge of my salvation, the remedy of my frailty and inconstancy, the reparation for all the defects of my life, and my secure refuge at the hour of my death. Be Thou, O Most Merciful Heart, my justification before God Thy Father, and screen me from His anger which I have so justly merited. I fear all from my own weakness and malice, but placing my entire confidence in Thee, O Heart of Love, I hope all from Thine infinite Goodness. Annihilate in me all that can displease or resist Thee. Imprint Thy pure love so deeply in my heart that I may never forget Thee or be separated from Thee.

I beseech Thee, through Thine infinite Goodness, grant that my name be engraved upon Thy Heart, for in this I place all my happiness and all my glory, to live and to die as one of Thy devoted servants.

Amen.

CHAPTER 8 - SAINT MICHAEL THE ARCHANGEL PRAYER (POPE LEO XIII) & SPIRITUAL DELIVERANCE PRAYERS

Pope Leo XIII had a vision during Mass that left him utterly stunned. According to one eyewitness:

Leo XIII truly saw, in a vision, demonic spirits who were congregating on the Eternal City (Rome).

(Father Domenico Pechenino, eyewitness; *Ephemerides Liturgicae*, reported in 1995, p. 58-59)

It is believed that the Pope overheard Satan asking the Lord for *a hundred years* to test the Church (which resulted in Leo XIII composing the prayer to St. Michael the Archangel).

St Michael the Archangel Prayer

St. Michael the Archangel,
defend us in battle.

Be our defense against the wickedness and snares of the Devil.

May God rebuke him, we humbly pray,
and do thou,
O Prince of the heavenly hosts,
by the power of God,
thrust into hell Satan,
and all the evil spirits,
who prowl about the world
seeking the ruin of souls. Amen.

Consecration Prayer to Saint Michael the Archangel

Oh most noble Prince of the Angelic Hierarchies, valorous warrior of Almighty God and zealous lover of His glory, terror of the rebellious angels, and love and delight of all the just angels, my beloved Archangel Saint Michael, desiring to be numbered among your devoted servants, I, today offer and consecrate myself to you, and place myself, my family, and all I possess under your most powerful protection. I entreat you not to look at how little, I, as your servant have to offer, being only a wretched sinner, but to gaze, rather, with favorable eye at the heartfelt affection with which this offering is made, and remember that if from this day onward I am under your patronage, you must during all my life assist me, and procure for me the pardon of my many grievous offenses, and sins, the grace to love with all my heart my God, my dear Savior Jesus, and my Sweet Mother Mary, and to obtain for me all the help necessary to arrive to my crown of glory. Defend me always from my spiritual enemies, particularly in the last moments of my life. Come then, oh Glorious Prince, and succor me in my last struggle, and with your powerful weapon cast far from me into the infernal abysses that prevaricator and proud angel that one day you prostrated in the celestial battle. Amen.

Daily Prayer to your
Guardian Angel

Angel of God, my guardian dear,
To whom God's love commits me here,
Ever this day be at my side,
To light and guard, to rule and guide.
Amen.

Prayers to Saint Raphael &
St Gabriel The Archangels

St Raphael
Healing Prayer

Glorious Archangel St. Raphael, great prince of the heavenly court, you are illustrious for your gifts of wisdom and grace. You are a guide of those who journey by land or sea or air, consoler of the afflicted, and refuge of sinners. I beg you, assist me in all my needs and in all the sufferings of this life, as once you helped the young Tobias on his travels. Because you are the "medicine of God" I humbly pray you to heal the many infirmities of my soul and the ills that afflict my body. I especially ask of you the favor (here mention your special intention), and the great grace of purity to prepare me to be the temple of the Holy Spirit. Amen.

St Gabriel Prayer

O blessed Archangel Gabriel, we beseech thee, do thou intercede for us at the throne of divine mercy in our present necessities, that as thou didst announce to Mary the mystery of the Incarnation, so through thy prayers and patronage in heaven we may obtain the benefits of the same, and sing the praise of God forever in the land of the living. Amen.

Remedy Against the "Spirits of Darkness" and the Forces of Hatred and Fear

August Queen of Heaven,

Sovereign Mistress of the Angels,
Thou Who from the beginning
has received from God the power and
mission to crush the head of Satan, we
humbly beseech Thee
to send Thy Holy Legions
that, under Thy command and by Thy
power,
they may pursue the evil spirits,
encounter them on every side,
resist their bold attacks
and drive them hence into the abyss of
eternal woe. Amen

Who Is Like unto God!
O good and tender Mother! Thou shalt
ever be our love and our hope.

O Mother of God, send the holy angels to
defend us and repel the cruel enemy far
from us.
Holy Angels and Archangels, keep us and
defend us. Amen

Indulgenced prayer. St. Pius X on 8 July 1908. Prayer dedicated by Our Lady to Fr. Cestac on 13 January 1864. It Is recommended to learn it by heart.

History of the Prayer

On 13 January 1864, Blessed Father Louis-Édouard Louis Cestac (founder of
the Congregation of the Servants of Mary, died in 1868), accustomed to the
goodness of the Most Blessed Virgin, was suddenly struck by a ray of divine
light. He saw devils scattered throughout the earth, causing inexplicable ravages. At the same time, he had a vision of the Most Blessed Virgin. This good Mother told him that indeed the devils were let loose in the world, and that the hour had come to pray to her as Queen of Angels, asking to send the Holy Legions to fight and put an end to the powers of Hell.

Imprimatur: Cameraci (Cambrai), 1912 A. Massart, Vicor General
(Source: https://catholicism.org/)

Demons of Discord, Depart!

During my night prayer, I experienced strong feelings of discord regarding some others. It was out of proportion with the events. It didn't make sense. Why am I so upset about nothing? It continued for quite some time.

Then it occurred to me....ah...demons of discord. So I repeated this deliverance prayer for about 15 minutes: "**Causa discordiae, vade! Causa discordiae, vade!**" (**Demons of discord, depart.**) It suddenly stopped and a feeling of harmony returned, confirming my discernment of a demonic influence.

Prayer Against Retaliation (Deliverance Prayer For the Laity to Recite)

Lord Jesus Christ, in your love and mercy, pour Your Precious Blood over us so that no demon or disembodied spirit may retaliate against us. Mary, surround us with your mantle, blocking any retaliating spirits from having any authority over us. St. Michael, surround us with your shield, so that no evil spirit may take revenge on us. Queen of Heaven and St. Michael, send

down the legions of angels under your command to fight off any spirits that would seek to harm us. All you saints of heaven, impede any retaliating spirit from influencing us. Lord, You are the Just Judge, the avenger of the wicked, the Advocate of the Just, we beg in Your mercy, that all we ask of Mary, the angels and the saints of heaven be also granted to all our loved ones, all of our possessions, those who pray for us and their loved ones, that for Your Glory's sake, we may enjoy Your perfect protection. Amen.

(Adapted from Chadd, Laity, p. 37)

(Source:https://www.catholicexorcism.org/ deliverance-prayers-for-the-laity)

CHAPTER 9- NOVENA OF ABANDONMENT & VENERABLE FATHER DOLINDO RUOTOLO

While inviting us to continually bring our worries and concerns to the Lord, Venerable Don Dolindo teaches us that the focus doesn't stay on our needs. He encourages us to bring our needs to God and then be at peace, leaving God free to care for us in his wisdom. Ven. Don Dolindo tells us that the Lord has promised to fully take on all the needs we entrust to him. In the words of Jesus to Don Dolindo:

Why do you confuse yourselves by worrying? Leave the care of your affairs to me and everything will be peaceful. I say to you in truth that every act of true, blind, complete surrender to me produces the effect that you desire and resolves all difficult situations. (...) **A thousand prayers do not equal one act of abandonment;** *don't ever forget it. There is no better novena than this:* **O Jesus, I abandon myself to you. Jesus, you take over.**

Incredible Prophecy from Fr. Dolindo given by Our Lady in 1921

The first form of mercy needed by this poor earth, and the Church first of all, is purification. Do not be frightened, do not fear, but it is necessary for a terrible hurricane to pass first over the Church and then the world!

The Church will almost seem abandoned and everywhere her ministers will desert her... even the churches will have to close! By his power the Lord will break all the bonds that now bind her [i.e. the Church] to the earth and paralyze her!

They have neglected the glory of God for human glory, for earthly prestige, for external pomp, and all this pomp will be swallowed up by a terrible, new persecution! Then we will see the value of human prerogatives and how it would have been better to lean on Jesus alone, who is the true life of the Church.

When you see the Pastors expelled from their seats and reduced to poor houses, when you see priests deprived of all their possessions, when you see external greatness abolished, say that the Kingdom of God is imminent! All this is mercy, not an ill!

Jesus wanted to reign by spreading His love and so often they have prevented Him from doing so. Therefore, he will disperse everything that is not his and will strike his ministers so that, deprived of all human support, they might live in Him alone and for Him!

This is the true mercy and I will not prevent what will seem to be a reversal but which is a great good, because I am the Mother of mercy!

The Lord will begin with His house and from there He will go on to the world...

Iniquity, having reached its apex, will fall apart and devour itself... (Source: https://www.markmallett.com/blog/ fr-dolinos-incredible-prophecy/)

The Prayer and Novena

The 'Prayer of Surrender' can be read in its entirety or prayed in nine shorter segments as a daily novena.

The Surrender Novena

Day 1

Why do you confuse yourselves by worrying? Leave the care of your affairs to me and everything will be peaceful. I say to you in truth that every act of true, blind, complete surrender to me produces the effect that you desire and resolves all difficult situations.

O Jesus, I surrender myself to you, take care of everything! (10 times)

Day 2

Surrender to me does not mean to fret, to be upset, or to lose hope, nor does it mean offering to me a worried prayer asking me to follow you and change your worry into prayer. It is against this surrender, deeply against it, to worry, to be nervous and to desire to think about the consequences of anything.

It is like the confusion that children feel when they ask their mother to see to their needs, and then try to take care of those needs for themselves so that their childlike efforts get in their mother's way. Surrender means to placidly close the eyes of the soul, to turn away from thoughts of tribulation and to put yourself in my care, so that only I act, saying, "You take care of it."

O Jesus, I surrender myself to you, take care of everything! (10 times)

Day 3

How many things I do when the soul, in so much spiritual and material need, turns to me, looks at me and says to me, "You take care of it," then closes its eyes and rests. In pain you pray for me to act, but that I act in the way you want. You do not turn to me, instead, you want me to adapt to your ideas. You are not sick people who ask the doctor to cure you, but rather sick people who tell the doctor how to. So do not act this way, but pray as I taught you in the Our Father: "Hallowed be thy Name," that is, be glorified in my need. "Thy kingdom come," that is, let all that is in us and in the world be in accord with your kingdom. "Thy will be done on Earth as it is in Heaven," that is, in our need, decide as you see fit for our temporal and eternal life. If you say to me truly: "Thy will be done," which is the same as saying: "You take care of it," I will intervene with all my omnipotence, and I will resolve the most difficult situations.

O Jesus, I surrender myself to you, take care of everything! (10 times)

Day 4

You see evil growing instead of weakening? Do not worry. Close your eyes and say to me with faith: "Thy will be done, You take care of it." I say to you that I will take care of it, and that I will intervene as does a doctor and I will accomplish miracles when they are needed. Do you see that the sick person is getting worse? Do not be upset, but close your eyes and say, "You take care of it." I say to you that I will take care of it, and that there is no medicine more powerful than my loving intervention. By my love, I promise this to you.

O Jesus, I surrender myself to you, take care of everything! (10 times)

Day 5

And when I must lead you on a path different from the one you see, I will prepare you; I will carry you in my arms; I will let you find yourself, like children who have fallen asleep in their mother's arms, on the other bank of the river. What troubles you and hurts you immensely are your reason, your thoughts and worry, and your desire at all costs to deal with what afflicts you.

O Jesus, I surrender myself to you, take care of everything! (10 times)

Day 6

You are sleepless; you want to judge everything, direct everything and see to everything and you surrender to human strength, or worse—to men themselves, trusting in their intervention—this is what hinders my words and my views. Oh, how much I wish from you this surrender, to help you; and how I suffer when I see you so agitated! Satan tries to do exactly this: to agitate you and to remove you from my protection and to throw you into the jaws of human initiative. So, trust only in me, rest in me, surrender to me in everything.

O Jesus, I surrender myself to you, take care of everything! (10 times)

Day 7

I perform miracles in proportion to your full surrender to me and to your not thinking of yourselves. I sow treasure troves of graces when you are in the deepest poverty. No person of reason, no thinker, has ever performed miracles, not even among the saints. He does divine works whosoever surrenders to God. So don't think about it any more, because your mind is acute and for you it is very hard to see evil and to trust in me and to not think of yourself. Do this for all your needs, do this, all of you, and you will see great continual silent miracles. I will take care of things, I promise this to you.

O Jesus, I surrender myself to you, take care of everything! (10 times)

Day 8

Close your eyes and let yourself be carried away on the flowing current of my grace; close your eyes and do not think of the present, turning your thoughts away from the future just as you would from temptation. Repose in me, believing in my goodness, and I promise you by my love that if you say, "You take care of it," I will take care of it all; I will console you, liberate you and guide you.

O Jesus, I surrender myself to you, take care of everything! (10 times)

Day 9

Pray always in readiness to surrender, and you will receive from it great peace and great rewards, even when I confer on you the grace of immolation, of repentance, and of love. Then what does suffering matter? It seems impossible to you? Close your eyes and say with all your soul, "Jesus, you take care of it." Do not be afraid, I will take care of things and you will bless my name by humbling yourself. A thousand prayers cannot equal one single act of surrender, remember this well. There is no novena more effective than this.

O Jesus, I surrender myself to you, take care of everything! (10 times)

Mother, I am yours now and forever.
Through you and with you
I always want to belong
completely to Jesus.

CHAPTER 10- THE DIVINE WILL & THE SERVANT OF GOD LUISA PICCARRETA

Jesus to the Luisa Piccarreta:

Ah, my daughter, the creature always races more into evil. How many machinations of ruin they are preparing! They will go so far as to exhaust themselves in evil. But while they occupy themselves in going their way, I will occupy Myself with the completion and fulfillment of My Fiat Voluntas Tua ("Thy will be done") so that My Will reign on earth—but in an all-new manner. Ah yes, I want to confound man in Love! Therefore, be attentive. I want you with Me to prepare this Era of Celestial and Divine Love. (February 8, 1921)

I anxiously await that My Will may be known and that the creatures may Live in It. Then, I will show off so much Opulence that every soul will be like a New Creation-Beautiful but distinct from all the others. I will amuse Myself; I will be her Insuperable Architect; I will display all My Creative Art … O, how I long for this; how I want it; how I yearn for it! Creation is not finished. I have yet to do My Most Beautiful Works. (February 7, 1938)

My daughter, when my Will has Its Kingdom upon earth and souls live in It, Faith will no longer have any shadow, no more enigmas, but everything will be clarity and certainty. The light of my Volition will bring in the very created things the clear vision of their Creator; creatures will touch Him with their own hands in everything He has done for love of them. (June 29, 1928)

On May 27, 1922, Jesus revealed to Luisa that the Prevenient Act, or the Morning Offering in the Divine Will, is made when the soul, at the first rising of the day, fixes her will in God's Will. Here the soul decides and confirms that she wants to live and operate only in God's Will. Thus, through this prayer a soul acts to achieve greater conformity to the Divine Will. (Luisa Piccarreta, The Book of Heaven, 1996)

The Prevenient Act, Or
The Morning Offering
in the Divine Will

"O Immaculate Heart of Mary, Mother and Queen of the Divine Will, I entreat you, by the infinite merits of the Sacred Heart of Jesus, and by the graces God has granted to you since your Immaculate Conception, the grace of never going astray.

Most Sacred Heart of Jesus, I am a poor and unworthy sinner, and I beg of you the grace to allow our Mother and Luisa to form in me the divine acts you purchased for me and for everyone. These acts are the most precious of all, for they carry the Eternal Power of your Fiat and they await my "Yes, your Will be done" (Fiat Voluntas Tua).

So I implore you, Jesus, Mary and Luisa to accompany me as I now pray:

I am nothing and God is all, come Divine Will. Come heavenly Father to beat in my heart and move in my Will; come beloved Son to flow in my blood and think in my intellect; come Holy Spirit to breath my lungs and recall in my memory. I fuse myself in the Divine Will and place my I love You, I adore You and I bless You God in the Fiats of

Creation. With my I love You my soul bilocates in the creations of the heavens and the earth: I love You in the stars, in the sun, in the moon and in the skies; I love You in the earth, in the waters and in every living creature my Father created out of love for me, so that I may return love for love.

I now enter into Jesus' Most Holy Humanity that embraces all acts. I place my I adore You Jesus in your every breath, heartbeat, thought, word and step. I adore You in the sermons of your public life, in the miracles you performed, in the Sacraments you instituted and in the most intimate fibers of your Heart.

I bless You Jesus in your every tear, blow, wound, thorn and in each drop of Blood that unleashed light for the life of every human. I bless You in all your prayers, reparations, offerings, and in each of the interior acts and pains you suffered up to your last breath on the Cross. I enclose your Life and all your acts, Jesus, with my I love You, I adore You and I bless You.

I now enter into the acts of my Mother Mary and of Luisa. I place my I thank you in Mary and Luisa's every thought, word and action. I thank you in the embraced joys and sorrows of Jesus' Redemption and of the Holy Spirit's Sanctification. Fused in your acts I make my I thank You and I bless You flow in the relations of every creature to fill their acts with light and life: to fill the acts of Adam and Eve; of the patriarchs and prophets; of the souls of the past, present and future; of the holy souls in purgatory; of the holy angels and saints.

I now make these acts my own, and I offer them to You, my tender and loving Father. May they increase the glory of your children, and may they glorify, satisfy and honor You on their behalf. Let us now begin our day with our Divine Acts fused together. Thank you Most Holy Trinity for enabling me to enter into union with You by means of prayer. May Your Kingdom come, and Your Will be done on earth as it is in Heaven."

Fiat!

(Source:https://www.ltdw.org)

The Command Prayer

Abba Father,
In the name of Jesus,
In the Unity and Power
of the Holy Spirit,
under the Mantle of Mary
with all the Angels and Saints
through the Intercession of
The Servant of God Luisa Piccarreta
take my humble prayer
and make it Your Command.
That all be accomplished and completed
In Your Most Holy Divine Will.
We Believe, We Receive.
FIAT! AMEN!

(*The Servant of God **LUISA PICCARRETA**
Little Daughter of the Divine Will*)

PRAYER OF CONSECRATION
TO THE DIVINE WILL

O adorable and Divine Will, here I am, before the immensity of Your Light, that Your Eternal Goodness may open to me the doors, and make me enter into It, to form my life all in You, Divine Will.

Therefore, prostrate before Your Light, I, the littlest among all creatures, come, O adorable Will, into the little group of the first children of Your Supreme Fiat. Prostrate in my nothingness, I beseech and implore Your endless Light, that It may want to invest me and eclipse everything that does not belong to You, in such a way that I may do nothing other than look, comprehend and live in You, Divine Will.

It will be my life, the center of my intelligence, the enrapturer of my heart and of my whole being. In this heart the human-will will no longer have life; I will banish it forever, and will form the new Eden of peace, of happiness and of love. With It I shall always be happy, I shall have a unique strength, and a sanctity that sanctifies everything and brings everything to God.

Here prostrate, I invoke the help of the Sacrosanct Trinity, that They admit me to live in the cloister of the Divine Will, so as to restore in me the original order of Creation, just as the creature was created.

Celestial Mother, Sovereign Queen of the Divine Fiat, take me by the hand and enclose me in the Light of the Divine Will. You will be my guide, my tender Mother; You will guard your child, and will teach me to live and to maintain myself in the order and in the bounds of the Divine Will. Celestial Sovereign, to your Heart I entrust my whole being; I will be the tiny little child of the Divine Will. You will teach me the Divine Will, and I will be attentive in listening to You. You will lay your blue mantle over me, so that the infernal serpent may not dare to penetrate into this Sacred Eden to entice me and make me fall into the maze of the human will.

Heart of my highest Good, Jesus, You will give me Your flames, that they may burn me, consume me and nourish me, to form in me the life of the Supreme Will.

Saint Joseph, You will be my Protector, the Custodian of my heart, and will keep the keys of my will in Your hands. You will keep my heart jealously, and will never give it to me again, that I may be sure never to go out of the Will of God.

Guardian Angel, guard me, defend me, help me in everything, so that my Eden may grow flourishing, and be the call of the whole world into the Will of God. Celestial Court, come to my help, and I promise You to live always in the Divine Will. **Amen.**

CONCLUDING PRAYER:
A PRAYER TO RECEIVE
THE FLAME OF LOVE

This prayer begins with a renewal of the Baptismal promises:

Do you renounce Satan? – I do.
Do you renounce all his works? – I do.
Do you renounce all his seductions? – I do.
Do you believe in God, the Father Almighty, Creator of heaven and earth? – I do.
Do you believe in Jesus Christ, His only Son, Our Lord, who was conceived by the power of the Holy Spirit, born of the Virgin Mary, suffered under Pontius Pilot, was crucified, died and was buried? – I do.

Do you believe that Jesus descended into hell; and on the third day rose from the dead, ascended into heaven and now sits at the right hand of God, the Father Almighty? – I do.

Do you believe in the Holy Spirit, the Holy Catholic Church, the Communion of Saints, the forgiveness of sins, the resurrection of the body, and life everlasting? – I do.

Imagine yourself clothed in white garments, a symbol of your Baptism and of your future life in heaven with the saints and angels.

Imagine an enormous Fire. You enter into that Fire. Do not be afraid. The Fire is Jesus Himself, The Flame of Love. You are not alone, Mary is with you. You are in the deepest part of Her Heart, immersed in her flame of love. Mary fills you with great desires so that you want to receive more and more of this Flame, surrender to the Flame and to have Him consume your whole life.

This Flame (Jesus himself) is the pearl of a great price, the treasure hidden in the field, the whole purpose of your life. Allow the Flame to enter your being. Allow Jesus to fill your imagination and memory. Close your eyes and imagine Jesus living within you.

Imagine Jesus in the mysteries of the rosary. He is conceived in Mary's womb. He sanctifies John the Baptist and Elizabeth. He is born into the world.

The shepherds and the Wise Men can see God's human face. At forty days, He fills the temple with light. At twelve, he fills that same temple with his teachings.

At 30, Jesus is baptized. He receives the Holy Spirit and hears the Father's voice. He changes water into wine. He preaches, heals, drives out demons and proclaims that the Kingdom is at hand. He reveals His full glory to Peter, James and John. On the night before His death, He says, "This is my Body," and "This is my blood."

He goes to the Garden where he accepts the Father's will. He gives Himself over to men whom Satan uses as his instruments. He accepts the wounds on His back and the thorns upon His head. He accepts the cross, walks to Calvary and dies for you.

His soul leaves His body and enters into eternal glory. Jesus' glorified soul re-enters His body, glorifies it and raises it from the dead. He appears to His disciples, tells them to make disciples of all nations, and ascends to the Father's right hand. He sends the Holy Spirit upon the disciples, takes His mother into heaven, body and soul, and then, makes her queen of all the angels and saints.

After imagining Jesus in these gospel stories, allow the flame to come to your will. You welcome Him and He enters your heart, you have invited Jesus to be the center of your life. He is your King. Place this fire on the lampstand and Jesus' light will flood you.

When you receive the Flame with others, you experience the communion of Saints. When one receives, all are blessed. When all receive, each is more blessed.

Right now, Our Lady embraces you and pours out her Flame of Love in great abundance. This is a holy and sacred moment. She sends this Flame into your heart. The Flame leaps from her heart to yours. She gives the Flame without limits. The Flame of Love is so great that She suffers until the Flame leaves Her Heart and goes to yours, because it belongs in our hearts. She gives the Fire far beyond your capacity to receive. She gives gifts that were meant for others but they did not receive. Receive this Flame for everyone – for yourself, your family, your friends. You will not realize all she has done for you this day. The effects will unfold slowly and powerfully.

Be still. The prayer is complete. Our Lady is pouring out the effects of grace of the Flame of Love. Remain in silence and receive. Be open to all that Jesus and Mary are doing within you.

(Source: https://flameoflove.us/a-prayer-to-pass-the-flame-of-love/)

Concluding Note

We hope that the prayers and devotions in this book will help you gain the graces and promises within. Please pray for our mission at Mother and Refuge of the End Times.

You can contact us on motheroftheendtimes@gmail.com

May God Bless and Protect You.

ABOUT THE AUTHOR

Mother And Refuge Of The End Times

Mother and Refuge of the End Times is made up of a group of lay and clerical volunteers who share the mission of spreading the messages of Heaven to the world. Our ministry consists of a YouTube Channel, prayer groups  on Telegram and other social media sites. We hope that this prayer book will be the first in a series of many to come. May God bless you and keep you!

Made in United States
Troutdale, OR
12/15/2023